*100 great recipes*

# Chinese

Ann Nicol

Published by SILVERDALE BOOKS
An imprint of Bookmart Ltd
Registered number 2372865
Trading as Bookmart Ltd
Blaby Road
Wigston
Leicester LE18 4SE

© 2005 D&S Books Ltd

D&S Books Ltd
Kerswell,
Parkham Ash, Bideford
Devon, England
EX39 5PR

e-mail us at:-
enquiries@d-sbooks.co.uk

This edition printed 2005

ISBN 1-84509-180-9

DS0114. 100 Great Chinese Recipes

Creative Director: Sarah King
Editor: Debbie Key
Project editor: Nicola Barber
Designer: Debbie Fisher
Photographer: Colin Bowling/Paul Forrester

Fonts: New York, Helvetica and Bradley Hand

Printed in China

1 3 5 7 9 10 8 6 4 2

# Contents

# introduction

# 100 great recipes
# Chinese

Chinese food is enjoyed by almost everyone in restaurants, but it is just as easy and fun to make, serve and eat at home. Choosing one hundred recipes for Chinese food to prepare and cook at home is a difficult job because there are so many delicious dishes to choose from. In *100 great recipes Chinese*, I have included a selection of quick and easy dishes made with the basics of chicken, beef, lamb, fish and vegetables. There is also a section on dishes for special occasions and buffets, and one on desserts.

Cooking in China is a tradition that goes back over thousands of years. This tradition has spread across the world and Chinese restaurant food is now widely available to all. Whilst everyone enjoys eating Chinese food, its preparation still appears a mystery and there is a belief that it is difficult and complicated to cook. The easy-to-follow, step-by-step recipes in this book will show you how simply and quickly you can achieve the tasty and authentic flavours and textures of Chinese food at home. Many of us lead busy lives and don't have time to cook complicated recipes, and most of us are also looking for a healthier lifestyle. The Chinese diet provides a solution: Chinese food is very healthy because it is produced by quick cooking methods which preserve nutrients, vitamins and minerals. Most Chinese cooking methods are already familiar to us, including boiling, poaching, grilling, steaming and deep-frying. Stir-frying is now a popular method for home cooking and means that finely cut ingredients can be cooked rapidly to contain their flavour, texture and nutrition.

Why does Chinese cooking transform ordinary everyday foods into delicious dishes? The major secret is the unusual way that contrasting tastes and textures, such as sweet and sour, soft and crisp, pungent and bland, are brought together. Chinese food is never bland and is always served with at least one flavouring. Contrast of flavour is fundamental to Chinese food, and the tastes of sweet, sour, bitter and salt, pungent or hot dishes need to be balanced.

Understanding the distinctive taste of Chinese food depends on using some special ingredients, without which it would lose its unique flavour. In Chinese seasoning, sugar is used more often than salt. Garlic, spring onions and ginger are introduced early in recipes to add zest to dishes. Fermented soya appears in many guises as beancurd, yellow bean sauce, barbecue and soy sauce. You will find that by adding sesame oil, oyster sauce or five-spice powder, you give the most ordinary foods a unique Oriental flavour.

# Serving Chinese Food

When planning a menu, harmony is the most important point to consider. Choose dishes that complement each other, but have a contrast in flavour, aroma, colour and texture. Serve one main dish per person, so that the more people eating, the more variety there is. Eating in China is a communal experience and all the dishes are meant to be shared between family and friends. A meal can consist of one meat dish, one fish and one vegetable dish served with a soup and a staple grain dish such as rice, noodles or dumplings. Use a variety of techniques to cook the dishes. For instance, serve a steamed dish, one braised dish and a stir-fried vegetable dish. Make one dish spicy, another hot and another delicate and mild. Make an effort to keep the textures different, for instance, one crisp deep-fried dish, one softly braised dish in a sauce and one crunchy vegetable dish. This variety of textures, flavours and colours will appeal to all the senses. Once you start to cook Chinese food regularly, you'll be amazed at your versatility, and you will soon find your own favourite dishes.

# Food Preparation

The major difference between European and Chinese food is the way it is prepared. Most Chinese dishes need to be cooked at high temperatures, very quickly, so need fine chopping and slicing. Once you have learned a few of the basic techniques, you will find Chinese food can be prepared easily and quickly.

In these recipes, metric quantities are given first, with imperial quantities second. Use one system or the other, because whilst both give excellent results, the amounts are not exactly the same.

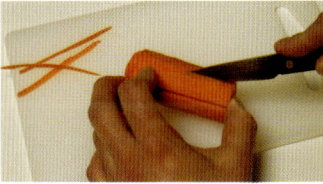

## Slicing

As stir-fried foods are cooked quickly, ingredients must be cut into very small pieces of equal size. Sliced foods may be cut into paper-thin slices, or cut meats across the grain and vegetables on the slant.

## Shredding

Place two or more slices or leaves of vegetables on top of one another and cut into matchstick strips.

## Dicing

Cut into 1cm/1/2 inch wide and thick strips, then cut across at 1cm/1/2 inch intervals to make cubes.

## Diagonal Cutting

Diagonal cutting is used to give vegetables such as celery and carrots a decorative finish. Make a diagonal cut straight down, then half turn and slice diagonally again to make a diamond shape.

# Cooking Methods

There are several cooking methods included in this book. You will find that in some recipes, you will need to combine a few of them.

## Simmering

Simmering in clear liquids such as stock adds flavour to soups. Crisp, shredded vegetables are usually added to simmered soups to add a crisp finish before serving.

## Steaming

Steaming is a healthy method of cooking as it uses very little fat and contains all the flavours, textures and goodness of foods. It is good for delicate fresh foods such as dumplings, fish and seafood and is widely used by Chinese cooks. The traditional bamboo steamers used in China, can be bought from Oriental stores and can be used to cook a whole meal at once. Rice, or the foods that take the longest to cook, are placed in the bottom steamer, then fish or meat in the next one and lightly shredded vegetables in the top compartment. If you don't have a bamboo steamer, use a heatproof plate placed on a trivet in the base of a large saucepan, surrounded by one-third boiling water, covered with a tightly fitting lid. Quickly steaming over a high heat for a short time gives best results.

# Grilling and Quick Roasting

Only marinated meats or good-quality, tender meats are suitable for this method of cooking. Meats should be high-roasted for a very short time only, to keep them succulent and juicy.

## Deep-frying

This can be done in a wok, or in a conventional deep-fat fryer. Dishes dipped in batters need to be deep-fried in hot oil in batches.

## Stir-frying

This is the most commonly known form of Chinese cooking, using a wok or large frying pan. Foods need to be chopped or sliced to a small size and quickly cooked over a fierce heat to preserve flavours and textures. A wok should be heated with a little vegetable or peanut oil before adding the ingredients. When adding the oil, swirl it around the heated wok to allow it to heat up quickly. When adding the first set of ingredients, reduce the heat a little to ensure they do not overcook. Use a long-handled scoop to allow you to turn the ingredients over so that they cook evenly. Once all the ingredients are added, increase the heat. This allows the food to cook in the quickest possible time and keeps their firm texture.

# Equipment

You can cook Chinese food using everyday items from the kitchen, but these basic ones will help to produce authentic results.

## Chopping Boards and Knives

A selection of good-quality chopping boards is vital for preparing Chinese food, as the basis of most recipes is chopping and cutting up ingredients.

## Cleaver

A cleaver is much heavier than an ordinary kitchen knife and this weight makes it ideal for chopping through bones or the shells of seafood. Cleavers are also ideal for fine shredding, chopping or crushing ginger and garlic. You will find a good-quality stainless steel cleaver with a fine, sharp blade invaluable for preparation.

## Food Processor

A small food processor or grinding mill is useful when preparing Chinese food, as it provides a super-quick alternative to chopping, grinding in a pestle and mortar, or beating by hand.

## Wooden Skewers

Bamboo skewers can be thrown away after use and are widely used for grilled foods. They need soaking before use to stop them from singeing.

# wok

The cone shape of a wok, with its rounded base, allows ingredients to be cooked in a minimum of fat. It maintains an intense heat steadily, the shape enabling the heat to spread evenly. Only a short cooking time is required so stir-fries retain freshness, texture and flavour and lose little of their nutritional value. Round-based, carbon steel woks, or Pau woks, are best suited to gas hobs where you can control the heat easily. Flat-based steel woks are best for electric, ceramic or solid fuel hobs, as they give a better distribution of heat. If you don't have a wok, a deep, heavy-based frying pan can make a reasonable substitute. Before using the wok for the first time, you will need to season it. To do this, heat the wok, add 3 tablespoons of salt and swirl around the pan for 10-15 minutes. Tip out the salt and wipe the wok with kitchen paper, then the wok is ready to use. A good, well-seasoned wok will create its own non-stick surface and needs little washing. Clean the wok by wiping the inside with kitchen paper. Keep washing with detergent to a minimum.

## Steamers

Bamboo steamers stack on top of one another and enable four or five dishes to be steamed at once. A tightly fitting lid is placed on top to prevent the steam from escaping. An ordinary stainless steel steamer or double boiler can be used if you don't have a traditional bamboo steamer. If you don't have a steamer, place the food on a heatproof plate on a rack 5cm/2 inches above the base of a pan of hot water and cover with foil, or a tightly fitting lid.

## Ladle

A large ladle is useful for spooning stock, soups or sauce into bowls.

## Pestle and Mortar

A stone pestle and mortar is useful for grinding small amounts of whole spices or herbs.

## A Draining Wire

This is a half-moon-shaped wire rack and is designed to sit on the side of a wok for draining foods and keeping them hot. It is used mainly for deep-frying.

## Skimmers

These are long-handled metal spatulas, shaped like small shovels, and they are used for scooping and tossing stir-fries in the wok. If you don't have a skimmer, use a long-handled spoon instead.

# Ingredients

Chinese food involves a number of specialist ingredients that give distinctive flavours and textures. You will find many of these in normal supermarkets, but a trip to an Oriental grocer or Chinese supermarket will prove interesting and you will find top-quality goods at very reasonable prices. You will find fresh ingredients on sale, but it is worthwhile building up a stock of frequently used ingredients for your store cupboard. Here are some of the essentials.

## Fresh Produce

**Baby sweetcorn cobs** These are colourful with a good crunchy texture and can be added whole or chopped into rings for stir-fries.

**Beancurd** Fresh beancurd is also known as tofu, or sometimes doufu in Chinese stores. Made from soya beans, it has a distinctive texture and is white in colour. It is rich in protein and highly nutritious. There are two types, a softer type often called silken tofu which can be used for soups, or a firmer cake type which can be used for cutting into strips or chunks for braises or stir-fries. The bland taste of tofu benefits from mixing with stronger ingredients and sauces, but it is delicate and needs careful cooking as it can disintegrate if over-stirred or cooked for too long.

**Beansprouts** These are the tiny crunchy shoots of mung beans. They are a very healthy vegetable, packed full of vitamins and minerals. They should be cooked for only a very short time to retain their crisp texture. Don't over-cook them as they will wilt.

**Chinese lettuce** The light green, tightly packed leaves of Chinese lettuce are crunchy, with a slightly sweet flavour. They can be eaten raw or cooked.

**Cucumbers** These are often used peeled and chopped, or sliced into fine matchsticks to garnish delicate dishes.

**Leeks** These make a good alternative to spring onions. Use them well-rinsed and sliced into very thin rings, or matchstick strips for stir-frying.

**Mangoes** Ripe mangoes make a wonderful addition to dessert dishes with their refreshing, sweet flavour. Look for ripe mangoes with a slight give in the flesh. Halve, remove the large stones, then peel to use and slice or cube.

**Pak choi** This is a flat, dark green leaf with a thick white vein in the centre. It has a mild, slightly peppery flavour and wilts down quickly on cooking. It is also known as bok choi or pok choi.

**Mushrooms** These are a popular ingredient in Chinese cooking. Choose oyster, shitake or brown cap mushrooms for braises or stir-fries. Ordinary, cultivated button mushrooms are cheaper but still as good to use as the more expensive, delicate varieties.

**Mooli** This is a giant white radish,
oblong in shape. Its crisp texture and delicate
flavour brings stir-fries alive. To prepare mooli, peel and cut
into 7.5cm/3 inch lengths, then slice or cut into matchsticks.

**Lychees** These are available fresh or in cans. Fresh lychees have a coarse, pink, papery skin
that is easy to peel away. They have a fragrant white fruit which surrounds a large brown stone.

**Spinach** Small spinach leaves wilt down and add colour and texture to braised dishes or stir-fries. Remove any large stems and wash the leaves in a few changes of cold water to remove
any sand or grit before use.

**Spring onions** Scallions or spring onions are commonly used in Chinese cooking. Both the
bulb and the leaves give a good flavour and both are useful and versatile for garnishes.

# Herbs and Spices

**Chillies** The powerful flavour and heat that fresh chillies provide in Chinese food is wonderful, but always bear in mind that fresh chillies must be handled with care. Remember that the hottest fresh chillies are usually the smallest in size. When the seeds are removed, this will reduce the heat. Do not let chilli flesh or juice touch your skin and do not rub your face or eyes after handling chillies. To prepare chillies, slice them in half lengthways and scoop out the seeds. You may wish to wear rubber gloves to protect your hands while doing this. Chop the chillies finely and wash your hands well after preparation.

**Coriander** Fresh coriander has a refreshing flavour and aroma. Remember to use the stalks as well as the leaves in cooking, as the stalks have a more concentrated flavour. Keep a bunch in a jug of cold water and it will store for up to five days in the refrigerator.

**Five-spice powder** This is an aromatic blend of cinnamon, cloves, star anise, peppercorns and fennel seeds. This spice blend is pungent and spicy with a slightly sweet flavour, and it has a spicy, exotic fragrance.

**Garlic** This is an essential seasoning in Chinese cookery and its highly aromatic taste and smell add a distinctive flavour. It can be used chopped, crushed or sliced. Look for fresh garlic which is firm and hard to the touch. Store it in a cool dry place, but not the fridge as it may become moist and start to sprout.

**Root ginger** This adds a warm, mellow heat to dishes. Look for the piece of ginger root with the smoothest skin as this will be the freshest and tastiest. The flesh should be firm and a creamy white colour if it is fresh. Ginger with wrinkled skin and yellow flesh will be old and have less flavour. To prepare, peel away the papery skin and use finely chopped, grated or sliced.

**Star anise** This star-shaped spice has an aniseed-like flavour. It can be used whole or can be ground, and it is good for marinated dishes.

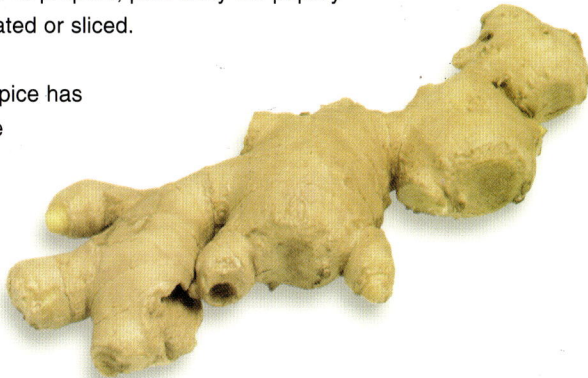

# From the Store Cupboard

**Bamboo shoots** These are the creamy coloured shoots of the bamboo plant and are crunchy in texture. They are available in cans and should be well-drained and rinsed before use.

**Bean sauces** These come in yellow and black varieties:

**Black beans** are very salty and need to be rinsed well before use if you are making your own sauce. You can buy a ready-made, thick, black bean sauce which is convenient for adding to stir-fries.

**Yellow beans** are soy beans and also very salty. Ready-made yellow bean sauce is thick and aromatic but is sweeter and more delicate than black bean sauce.

**Cornflour** This is an invaluable ingredient in Chinese cooking as it can be used to thicken sauces and marinades. It can bind minced meats or stuffings together and also coat delicate foods to help seal in flavour and texture. Before adding to sauces, it should be blended with a little cold water to make a smooth, even paste.

**Dried beancurd** Made from dehydrated pureed soy bean cakes, it is available in packets and needs to be soaked overnight in cold water, or for 1 hour in warm water, to rehydrate it before using.

**Dried mushrooms** These are available in Oriental stores in plastic bags. They will keep almost indefinitely in an airtight container. They need to be soaked in warm water for 20 minutes before use and have a delicate fragrance.

**Hoisin sauce** This is a thick, dark brown soy-based sauce made with sugar, spices, garlic and chilli and is slightly sweet. It can be used as a dip or in stir-fries and is sold in jars or cans. Once opened, store in the refrigerator.

**Noodles** There are several varieties of noodles used in Chinese cooking:

*Yellow dried-egg noodles* are easily available and are sold in thick ribbons, or medium or thin strands.

*Rice noodles* are sometimes known as cellophane noodles because they are white and semi-transparent in colour. They need to be soaked in water for 5 minutes before use to allow them to expand.

**Oils** Most Chinese recipes include the cooking medium of oil. Groundnut or peanut oil is best for stir-frying as it can be heated to a high temperature. It is available in Oriental stores, but if you cannot get this, sunflower oil makes the best substitute as it is light in colour and flavour. Avoid heavy oils such as olive oil for Chinese cooking.

**Oyster sauce** This is a thin, light brown sauce made from oysters and soy sauce. It is available in bottles and is used for delicately flavouring meat and fish dishes. Once opened, store the bottle in the refrigerator.

**Red chilli sauce** Hot chilli sauce is bright red and made from chillies, sugar, vinegar and salt. It can be used for cooking or as a dipping sauce. Red chilli sauce is available from Oriental food stores in different strengths, so it is worth trying several for the degree of heat that you prefer.

**Rice wine** Similar to dry sherry in flavour, the best brands come from Shaoxing in eastern China. As only small amounts are used, it is worth buying for its distinctive flavour. If you cannot buy rice wine, use dry sherry as the best substitute.

**Vinegars** Chinese rice vinegars add an authentic flavour to dishes. There are three varieties all with a distinctive taste:

*White rice vinegar* is light in colour and transparent and has a mild delicate, distinctive sweet taste.

*Red rice vinegar* is deep red and has a thin texture. It is spicy in taste and can be used in cooking or as a dipping sauce for seafood.

*Black rice vinegar* is very dark brown in colour and thick in texture. It is mild in flavour and useful for braised dishes.

**Sesame seeds** These are tiny, flat seeds which are often roasted and sprinkled over both sweet and savoury dishes.

**Sesame seed oil** A nutty flavoured aromatic oil. As it burns easily, it usually added to dishes just before serving. Made from roasted sesame seeds and sold in small bottles, it is used as a seasoning and flavouring rather than for cooking and should not be used for frying on its own.

**Soy sauce** This comes in two varieties, light and dark. The darker form is stronger and thicker and gives a rich colour to foods. The lighter one is more delicate and can be used with fish or vegetables or as an accompaniment or dip. It is worth buying the most expensive products as these are better grades of sauce.

**Spring roll and wonton wrappers** These are wafer-thin pastry wrappers made from a flour and water dough. They can be filled with minced meat or chopped vegetables to make spring rolls. Wonton wrappers are made from an egg and flour dough and are sold fresh or frozen, packed as small stacks of yellow squares. You can buy both fresh or frozen packs from Oriental grocers and supermarkets. To use the wrappers, peel away the number that you need and freeze the rest, wrapped in clingfilm.

**Sichuan pepper** This is available as ground or whole peppercorns and is very hot and spicy. Use sparingly for marinating and cooking.

**Water chestnuts** These are small, white, flat rounds sold ready-peeled in cans. They are deliciously crisp and crunchy in texture with a delicate, slightly sweet flavour.

# Tips for Successful Cooking

- Use metric or imperial measurements only; do not mix the two.

- Use measuring spoons: 1 tsp = 5ml; 1tbsp = 15ml

- All spoon measurements are level unless otherwise stated.

- All eggs are medium unless otherwise stated.

- Recipes using raw or lightly cooked eggs should not be given to babies, pregnant woman, the very old or anyone suffering from or recovering from an illness.

- The cooking times are an approximate guide only. If you are using a fan oven reduce the cooking time according to the manufacturer's instructions.

- Ovens should be preheated to the required temperature.

- Fruits and vegetables should be washed before use.

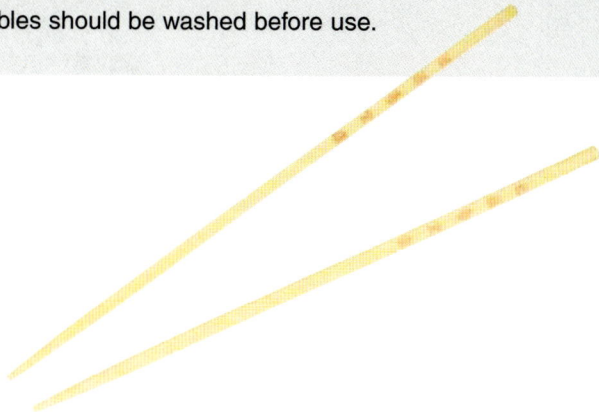

# soups *and* starters

# Hot & Sour Soup

*Hot and spicy*

This traditional soup has become a favourite in Chinese restaurants.

## Ingredients for 2

500ml/18 fl oz chicken stock
1/2 tbsp cornflour
1 tbsp Chinese red rice
    vinegar
1 tbsp light soy sauce
25g/1oz open mushrooms,
    sliced
50g/2oz ham, shredded
25g/1oz beansprouts
1 spring onion, finely
    chopped
1 clove garlic, peeled and
    chopped
1 green chilli, seeded and
    thinly sliced
1/2 tsp soft light brown sugar
2 tsp sesame oil
1 egg, beaten
1 tbsp rice wine

## Ingredients for 4

1 litre/1 3/4 pints chicken stock
1 tbsp cornflour
2 tbsp Chinese red rice
    vinegar
2 tbsp light soy sauce
50g/2oz open mushrooms,
    sliced
100g/4oz ham, shredded
50g/2oz beansprouts
2 spring onions, finely
    chopped
1 clove garlic, peeled and
    chopped
2 green chillies, seeded and
    thinly sliced
1 tsp soft light brown sugar
1 tbsp sesame oil
2 eggs, beaten
2 tbsp rice wine

1 Bring the stock to the boil in a large pan. Mix the cornflour to a paste with the vinegar, soy sauce and 1 tablespoon of water.

2 Stir the paste into the stock and cook over a high heat, stirring until the liquid thickens.

3 Add all the remaining ingredients (except the eggs and the wine) and simmer for 5 minutes.

4 Gradually trickle in the beaten egg in a continuous stream, stirring to create threads of egg. Add the wine and pour into warmed bowls. Serve immediately.

# Crab & Sweetcorn Soup

*Low Fat*

You can make this soup ahead of time as it reheats well.

## Ingredients for 2

600ml/1 pint chicken stock
150g/5oz frozen sweetcorn
    kernels
2 tsp rice wine
2 tsp light soy sauce
1 tsp cornflour
1cm/1/2 inch root ginger,
    peeled and finely
    chopped
1/2 tsp salt
1/2 tsp caster sugar
100g/4oz canned white
    crabmeat
1/2 egg white
1 tsp sesame oil

## Ingredients for 4

1.2 litres/2 pints chicken
    stock
250g/9oz frozen sweetcorn
    kernels
1 tbsp rice wine
1 tbsp light soy sauce
2 tsp cornflour
2.5cm/1 inch root ginger,
    peeled and finely
    chopped
1 tsp salt
1 tsp caster sugar
225g/8oz canned white
    crabmeat
1 egg white
1 tsp sesame oil

1 Bring the chicken stock to the boil in a large pan, add the sweetcorn and simmer for 10 minutes.

2 Blend the rice wine, soy sauce and cornflour with 1 tablespoon of water and add to the pan with the ginger, salt and sugar, stirring.

3 Bring back to the boil, then reduce to a simmer and add the crabmeat.

4 Mix the egg white and sesame oil in a bowl, then slowly pour into the hot soup in a stream, stirring continuously. Serve immediately in warmed bowls garnished with fried shallots.

# Chicken Noodle Soup

*Easy Entertaining*

Serve this simple soup as a starter or as a light meal.

## Ingredients for 2

500ml/18fl oz chicken stock
100g/4oz chicken breast
2 spring onions finely sliced
1cm/½ inch root ginger,
     peeled and finely
     chopped
½ tsp sesame oil
50g/2oz fine egg noodles
1 tbsp fresh coriander,
     chopped
Salt to taste

## Ingredients for 4

1 litre/1¾ pints chicken
     stock
225g/8oz chicken breast
4 spring onions finely sliced
2.5cm/1 inch root ginger,
     peeled and finely
     chopped
1 tsp sesame oil
100g/4oz fine egg noodles
1 tbsp fresh coriander,
     chopped
Salt to taste

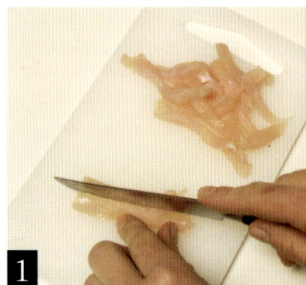

1 Bring the chicken stock to the boil in a large pan. Remove any skin and bones from the chicken and slice into thin strips.

2 Add the chicken meat, sliced spring onions, ginger and sesame oil to the stock and simmer for 10 minutes.

3 Add the noodles and stir to separate them. Simmer for 5 minutes.

4 Add the fresh coriander and stir. Season with salt and taste the soup. Simmer for 2-3 minutes then pour into warmed bowls and serve immediately.

# Tricolour Soup

*vegetarian*

This soup is so-called because it is based on three colours, red white and green.

## Ingredients for 2

600ml/1 pint vegetable stock
100g/4oz fresh ripe beefsteak
  tomatoes
100g/4oz beancurd
100g/4oz fresh leaf spinach
  or Chinese leaf
2 tsp dark soy sauce
1/2 tsp white rice vinegar

## Ingredients for 4

1.2 litres/2 pints vegetable
  stock
225g/8oz fresh ripe beefsteak
  tomatoes
225g/8oz beancurd
225g/8oz fresh leaf spinach
  or Chinese leaf
1 tbsp dark soy sauce
1 tsp white rice vinegar

1 Place the stock in a large pan and bring to the boil.

2 Cut the tomatoes in half, scoop out the seeds and cut the flesh into thin slices.

3 Slice the beancurd into 1 cm/1/2 inch cubes, cutting with a sharp knife as the curd will crumble easily.

4 Add the tomatoes and curd to the stock with the spinach leaves, and simmer for 3-4 minutes until the leaves have wilted. Stir in the soy sauce and vinegar, simmer for 1 minute, then serve.

# Eggflower Soup

## Low Fat

This soup is so-called because of the delicate pattern the eggs make when they are swirled into the soup.

### Ingredients for 2

**600ml/1 pint vegetable stock**
**½ tsp caster sugar**
**½ tsp salt**
**2 tsp dark soy sauce**
**100g/4oz fresh tomatoes, finely chopped**
**2 spring onions**
**1 egg**
**1 tsp sesame oil**

### Ingredients for 4

**1.2 litres/2 pints vegetable stock**
**1 tsp caster sugar**
**1 tsp salt**
**1 tbsp dark soy sauce**
**225g/8oz fresh tomatoes, finely chopped**
**3 spring onions**
**2 eggs**
**2 tsp sesame oil**

1 Place the stock in a large pan and bring to the boil. Add the sugar, salt, soy sauce and tomatoes and simmer for 5 minutes.

2 Slice the spring onions finely and add the white part to the pan. Simmer for 5 minutes.

3 Whisk the eggs and the sesame oil together with a fork.

4 Stir the egg mixture into the soup in a thin, slow, stream. Using a fork, separate the egg mixture into strands. Serve in warmed bowls garnished with the green sliced spring onion.

# Prawn Toasts

*Quick and Easy*

Serve these hot, delicate prawn toasts as part of a platter full of mixed starters.

## Ingredients for 2

**100g/4oz prawns**
**1 spring onion, chopped**
**1 tsp light soy sauce**
**2 tsp fresh coriander,**
    **chopped**
**1 clove garlic, peeled,**
    **chopped**
**1 tsp sesame oil**
**2 tsp cornflour**
**1/2 egg white, beaten**
**2 slices white bread**
**2 tsp sesame seeds**
**Vegetable oil for deep frying**

## Ingredients for 4

**225g/8oz prawns**
**1 spring onion, chopped**
**1 tbsp light soy sauce**
**1 tbsp fresh coriander,**
    **chopped**
**1 clove garlic, peeled,**
    **chopped**
**1 tsp sesame oil**
**1 tbsp cornflour**
**1 egg white, beaten**
**3-4 slices white bread**
**4 tsp sesame seeds**
**Vegetable oil for deep frying**

1 Place the prawns, spring onion, soy sauce, coriander and garlic into a food processor and process until finely minced. Alternatively, chop by hand until fine.

2 Blend the oil, cornflour and egg white and stir until a thick paste blends together. Add the chopped vegetables and prawns.

3 Remove the crusts from the bread and spread the mixture onto one side of each slice. Sprinkle the sesame seeds over the top of the mixture and press on.

4 Heat the oil in a deep fat fryer and fry the slices for about 5 minutes until golden. Drain on kitchen paper and cut each piece into thin slices to serve.

# Spring Rolls

*Family Favourite*

The pastry for spring rolls is paper thin and crispy when fried. You can buy spring roll wrappers frozen from Chinese stores, then make your own delicious fillings.

## Ingredients for 4

**20 spring roll pastry skins each 25cm/10 inch square or Greek filo pastry**

### Filling

**1 tbsp sesame oil**
**1 clove garlic, finely chopped**
**1cm/½ inch root ginger, peeled and grated**
**1 spring onion, finely chopped**
**25g/1oz carrot, finely grated**
**25g/1oz mooli, finely shredded**
**25g/1oz beansprouts**
**1 tbsp hoisin sauce**
**100g/4oz char sui barbecued pork, shredded, or minced pork**
**Vegetable oil for deep fat frying**
**Chilli dipping sauce to serve**

1 Heat the sesame oil in a wok or frying pan, add the ginger, garlic and spring onions and stir-fry for 1-2 minutes.

2 Add the carrot, beansprouts and mooli and stir-fry for 2 minutes. Add the pork and hoisin sauce and stir fry for 3-4 minutes. Spoon the ingredients into a bowl to cool.

3 Lay a sheet of spring roll pastry onto a flat surface. Place 2 tablespoons of filling at one end of the sheet, then roll the sheet over the filling. Fold the sides in over the filing. Roll up, leaving a small edge of pastry. Dampen this with water and finish rolling up to seal.

4 Fill a deep-fat fryer with oil and heat to 180°C/350°F. Place 4 spring rolls in the frying basket and deep-fry for 6-8 minutes until golden. Drain on kitchen paper and serve hot with chilli dipping sauce.

# Sesame Chicken Wings

*Easy Entertaining*

These sticky little winglets are great to serve with drinks, as they can be easily eaten with your fingers.

## Ingredients for 2

**4 chicken wing joints**
**2 tsp salted black beans**
**2 tsp vegetable oil**
**1 clove garlic, crushed**
**1cm/¹/₂ inch root ginger,**
   **peeled and grated**
**1 tbsp dark soy sauce**
**2 tsp rice wine or dry sherry**
**Black pepper**
**1 tbsp sesame seeds**

## Ingredients for 4

**8 chicken wing joints**
**1 tbsp salted black beans**
**1 tbsp vegetable oil**
**1 clove garlic, crushed**
**2cm/³/₄ inch root ginger,**
   **peeled and grated**
**2 tbsp dark soy sauce**
**1 tbsp rice wine or dry sherry**
**Black pepper**
**2 tbsp sesame seeds**

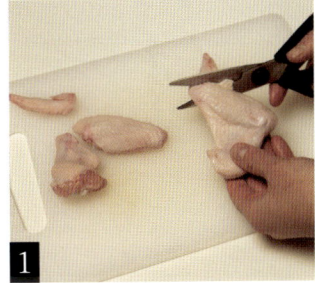

1 Trim off the wing tips and cut each chicken piece in two at the joint. Crush or process the beans with 1 tablespoon of water.

2 Heat the oil in a wok, or large frying pan and stir-fry the garlic and ginger for 1-2 minutes. Add the chicken wings and stir-fry for 3-4 minutes until browned.

3 Add the soy sauce, wine or sherry, beans and a large pinch of black pepper. Cover and simmer for 1-2 minutes.

4 Uncover the pan and turn up the heat. Continue cooking until all the liquid has evaporated and the chicken pieces have a sticky glaze. Remove to a serving plate and sprinkle with sesame seeds. Serve hot.

# Satay Sticks

*Low Fat*

Satay originally comes from Indonesia, but you will find it on the menu in many Chinese restaurants now.

## Ingredients for 2

**225g/8oz chicken breasts**

### Marinade:

**1 tbsp peanut butter**
**1 tbsp rice wine or dry sherry**
**2 tsp light soy sauce**
**1 tsp chilli sauce**
**1/2 tsp medium curry powder**
**4 bamboo skewers, soaked**
    **in water for 30 minutes**
**Chilli dipping sauce**

## Ingredients for 4

**450g/1lb chicken breasts**

### Marinade:

**2 tbsp peanut butter**
**2 tbsp rice wine or dry sherry**
**1 tbsp light soy sauce**
**1 tbsp chilli sauce**
**1 tsp medium curry powder**
**8 bamboo skewers, soaked**
    **in water for 30 minutes**
**Chilli dipping sauce**

1 Remove skin and bones from the chicken and cut it into 1cm/1/2 inch cubes. Mix all the marinade ingredients together.

2 Place the marinade in a bowl, add the chicken and toss to coat it. Cover and chill for 2 hours, or up to 24 hours in the fridge.

3 Heat the grill to medium hot. Thread the chicken onto the soaked skewers, leaving a little space between the pieces.

4 Cook under the grill for about 5 minutes, turning the skewers occasionally. Serve with chilli dipping sauce.

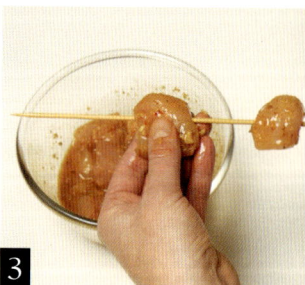

# Butterfly Prawns

## Easy Entertaining

This dish is so-called because of the shape that is formed when the prawns are split and flattened.

### Ingredients for 2

**4 raw giant king prawns or tiger prawns**

#### For the batter:

**2 tbsp cornflour**
**1 tbsp plain flour**
**2 egg whites**
**Vegetable oil for deep-fat frying**
**Chilli dipping sauce to serve**

### Ingredients for 4

**8 raw giant king prawns or tiger prawns**

#### For the batter:

**4 tbsp cornflour**
**2 tbsp plain flour**
**4 egg whites**
**Vegetable oil for deep-fat frying**
**Chilli dipping sauce to serve**

1 Make the batter. Sift the flours together into a bowl with a pinch of salt. Whisk together with the egg whites and set aside.

2 Peel the prawns, leaving the tails on. Make a shallow cut along the back of each prawn with the tip of a sharp knife and remove the black vein.

3 Cut down the front of each prawn, being careful not to cut right through the flesh. Place the prawn on a flat surface and press out gently to make a butterfly shape.

4 Heat the oil in a deep fat fryer to 190°C/375°F. Dip each prawn in batter to coat, then cook in the hot oil for 3-4 minutes.

# dim sum
## and
# extras

# Mini Spare Ribs

## Hot and spicy

These sticky morsels are delicious served with drinks or as part of a mixed starter plate.

### Ingredients for 2

**225g/8oz small pork spare ribs**
**2 tbsp hoisin sauce**
**2 tsp chilli and garlic sauce**
**2 tsp yellow rice wine**
**Spring onion tassels to garnish**

### Ingredients for 4

**450g/1lb small pork spare ribs**
**6 tbsp hoisin sauce**
**1 tbsp chilli and garlic sauce**
**1 tbsp yellow rice wine**
**Spring onion tassels to garnish**

1 If the ribs are large, cut them in half with a meat cleaver. Place the ribs in a dish.

2 Mix the hoisin sauce, chilli, garlic sauce and rice wine together, pour over the ribs and leave to marinate in the fridge for at least 3 hours.

3 Heat the oven to 190°C/375°F/Gas 5. Place the ribs in a lightly oiled meat roasting dish and drizzle over any remaining sauce.

4 Bake for 30-40 minutes, or until tender with a dark brown sticky coating. Serve immediately.

# Crispy Crab Wontons

## Easy Entertaining

These delicious little nibbles have a crisp, crunchy finish.

### Ingredients for 2

**12 wonton wrappers**

#### Filling:

**40g/ 1¹/₂ oz canned white crabmeat**
**40g/ 1¹/₂ oz cod, skinned and boned**
**¹/₂ small green chilli, finely chopped**
**1 spring onion, finely chopped**
**¹/₂ tsp cornflour**
**1 tsp light soy sauce**
**Vegetable oil for deep frying**
**Chilli dipping sauce to serve**

### Ingredients for 4

**24 wonton wrappers**

#### Filling:

**75g/3oz canned white crabmeat**
**75g/3oz cod, skinned and boned**
**1 small green chilli, finely chopped**
**1 spring onion, finely chopped**
**1 tsp cornflour**
**1 tbsp light soy sauce**
**Vegetable oil for deep frying**
**Chilli dipping sauce to serve**

1 Place all the filling ingredients into a food processor or mincer and blend to a coarse puree.

2 Dust a work surface with flour. Spread out each wonton wrapper flat and place a teaspoon of filling in the centre of each one.

3 Dampen the edges of the pastry and fold over to form a triangle. Press the

edges together, then fold them round towards the centre and pinch them together.

4 Heat the oil in a deep fat fryer or deep wok to 190°C/375°F. Fry the wontons in batches, allowing enough room for them to move around and cook on all sides. Deep-fry for 4-6 minutes until puffy and golden. Drain, then place on kitchen paper for a few moments and serve piping hot.

# Crispy Fried Pancake Rolls

## Easy Entertaining

These long cigar-shaped starters can be prepared well ahead of time, then fried and served crisp and piping hot.

### Ingredients for 2

2 tsp sunflower oil
1 spring onion, finely
    chopped
1 clove garlic, chopped
100g/4oz minced pork
50g/2oz canned water
    chestnuts, drained
50g/2oz pak choi
2 tsp soy sauce
4 x 25cm/10 inch spring roll
    wrappers
Vegetable oil for deep frying
Chilli sauce for dipping

### Ingredients for 4

1 tbsp sunflower oil
2 spring onions, finely
    chopped
1 clove garlic, chopped
225g/8oz minced pork
100g/4oz canned water
    chestnuts, drained
100g/4oz pak choi
4 tsp soy sauce
8 x 25cm/10 inch spring roll
    wrappers
Vegetable oil for deep frying
Chilli sauce for dipping

1 Heat the oil in a wok or large frying pan. Add the onion and garlic and stir-fry for 1 minute. Add the minced pork and fry for 3-4 minutes to brown.

2 Finely chop or process the water chestnuts and shred the pak choi leaves as thinly as possible. Add to the pork in the pan with the soy sauce and stir fry for 2-3 minutes until the leaves have wilted. Cool.

3 Spread out each spring roll wrapper and spoon 2 tablespoons of filling along one edge. Roll the wrapper over once, and tuck in the sides. Roll up completely to make a sausage shape, then brush the long edge lightly with water and press to seal.

4 Heat the oil in a deep-fat fryer or wok and fry in batches for 3-4 minutes. Remove with a slotted spoon and drain on kitchen paper. Serve hot with chilli sauce.

# Rice Paper Squares

## Easy Entertaining

Dim sum – a selection of small, tasty delicacies – are served as snacks, starters or can be eaten as a light meal

### Ingredients for 2

½ egg white
1 tsp cornflour
1 tsp rice wine or dry sherry
1 tsp hoisin sauce
100g/4oz cooked prawns,
　(thawed if frozen)
2 spring onions, finely
　shredded
4 rice paper wrappers
Vegetable oil for deep frying
Plum sauce to serve

### Ingredients for 4

1 egg white
2 tsp cornflour
2 tsp rice wine or dry sherry
2 tsp hoisin sauce
225g/8oz cooked prawns
　(thawed if frozen)
4 spring onions, finely
　shredded
8 rice paper wrappers
Vegetable oil for deep frying
Plum sauce to serve

1 Beat the egg white with the cornflour, wine or sherry and hoisin sauce. Chop the prawns in half and add to the mix with the spring onions.

2 Dip the rice paper wrappers in a dish of water, one at a time to soften them. Spread them out flat on a work surface.

3 Divide the mixture and spoon into the centre of each wrapper. Bring two sides up over the filling, then the other two sides over to make a square parcel.

4 Heat the oil in a wok or deep-fat fryer and deep-fry the squares in small batches for about 3 minutes until crisp and light golden. Drain on kitchen paper. Serve with plum sauce for dipping.

# Pickled Vegetables

Low Fat

A jar of pickled vegetables is regularly made in most Chinese households for serving with hot, savoury dishes.

## Makes 900g/2lb pickled vegetables:

350g/12oz carrots
350g/12oz mooli, or small white turnips
225g/8oz pak choi
2 red chillies

## For the pickling liquid:

50g/2oz salt
90ml/3fl oz rice wine or dry sherry
75g/3oz caster sugar
5cm/2 inch root ginger, peeled and grated
2 large cloves garlic, chopped

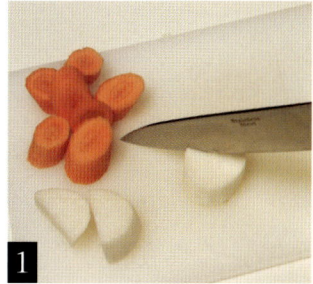

1 Peel the carrots and mooli or turnips and slice into 2.5cm/1 inch chunks.

2 Cut the leaves into 2.5cm/1 inch thick slices. Slice the chillies thinly, retaining the seeds.

3 Mix all the pickling liquid ingredients together and place in a large glass or pottery bowl and stir until the sugar and salt have dissolved. Don't use a metal bowl.

4 Add the sliced vegetables, stir, cover and refrigerate for 3-5 days. The longer they remain in the liquid, the saltier they will taste.

5 Drain the vegetables and rinse well in cold water. Store in a sealed plastic container in the fridge until needed.

# Prawn Crackers

## Easy Entertaining

Prawn crackers can be bought from Chinese supermarkets for deep-frying at home. They are sold in boxes as small, thin, transparent, flat discs made from rice flour and shrimp powder. When they are deep-fried they fluff up to double their size to a light, crunchy, crisp texture that we all love.

### Ingredients for 2

**8 dry, uncooked prawn crackers**
**Vegetable oil for deep-frying**

### Ingredients for 4

**16 dry, uncooked prawn crackers**
**Vegetable oil for deep-frying**

1 Heat the oil in a deep fat fryer, or a deep wok, to a temperature of 190°C/375°F, or, if you have an electric deep fryer, set it to potato chip frying temperature.

2 Add the prawn crackers to the frying basket or wok in small batches. Don't be tempted to overload the basket, as the crackers will double or treble in size, expanding very quickly.

3 Fry each batch of crackers for about 10 seconds, until puffed up and white.

4 Spread each batch of cooked crackers out onto a tray lined with absorbent kitchen paper to drain and crisp.

5 Serve the crackers immediately, warm, or cool and store in an airtight tin for up to 1 week.

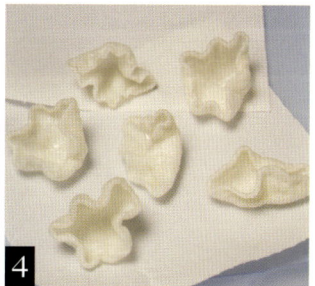

# Chinese Pancakes

*Family Favourite*

Chinese pancakes are needed for serving rolled, filled, savoury pancake dishes, such as Peking duck. You can buy them ready made in supermarkets, but they are much cheaper to make at home and you will never run out of them.

## Makes 18 pancakes

**125ml/4fl oz boiling water**
**175g/6oz plain flour**
**3 tbsp sesame oil**

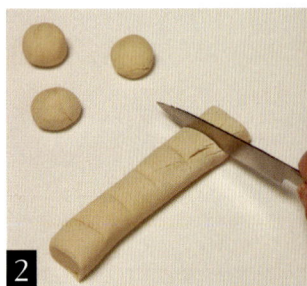

1 Sift the flour into a bowl, add the boiling water and mix to a soft dough. Place on a floured surface and knead well. Cover with a damp cloth and set aside for 30 minutes.

2 Roll the dough into a long sausage 2.5cm/1 inch wide. Cut into 18 pieces and roll each piece into a ball.

3 Lightly dust the surface with flour. Flatten each ball with a rolling pin and roll out into a 6cm/2½ inch round.

4 Brush one side of each pancake lightly with sesame oil. Place two pancakes together, oiled sides touching. Lightly dust with flour and roll with a rolling pin to make 12.5cm/5 inch pancakes.

5 Heat a heavy-based frying pan over a medium heat. Cook the doubled pancakes in the dry pan. When the dough bubbles, turn over and cook for 1 minute. Pull the pancakes apart into two and stack on a plate, separated with greaseproof paper. Cover and keep warm.

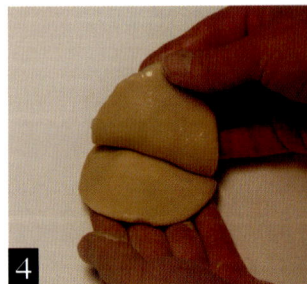

# Crispy Seaweed

*vegetarian*

Chinese crispy seaweed is not actually made from seaweed but from Chinese cabbage, pak choi, sometimes known as bok choi or pok choi.

## Ingredients for 2

**450g/1lb pak choi**
**Vegetable oil for deep-frying**
**½ teaspoon salt**
**1 tsp caster sugar**

## Ingredients for 4

**900g/2lb pak choi**
**Vegetable oil for deep-frying**
**1 teaspoon salt**
**2 tsp caster sugar**

1 Preheat the oven to 130°C/250°F/Gas ½. Cut away the white veins and stalks from the cabbage and discard. Wash the green leaves that are left in cold water and drain thoroughly.

2 Roll up a few leaves into cigarette shapes and shred them as finely as possible. Spread them out onto baking sheets and dry for 10 minutes only. Do not allow them to dry completely, or else the cabbage will burn when it is fried. Remove from the oven to cool.

3 Heat the oil in a deep-fat fryer or wok until hot. Add the shredded leaves in two or three batches and fry for about 30 seconds, when they will turn dark green.

4 Spread the fried leaves out on kitchen paper and cool. Toss in the salt and sugar and serve in small bowls.

# Pot Sticker Dumplings

*Easy Entertaining*

These little delicacies take a little time to make, but they are well worth the trouble.

## Makes 16

**175g/6oz plain flour**
**4 tbsp vegetable oil**
**90ml/3fl oz boiling water**
**150ml/¹/₄ pint chicken stock**
**Chilli or plum dipping sauce**

## Filling:

**150g/5oz Chinese barbecue pork, finely chopped**
**25g/1oz white cabbage, finely chopped**
**2 spring onions, finely chopped**
**¹/₂ small green pepper, finely chopped**
**1 tbsp light soy sauce**
**1 tbsp rice wine or dry sherry**
**1 tsp sesame oil**
**¹/₂ tsp caster sugar**

1 Sift the flour into a bowl and make a well in the centre. Add the boiling water and 2 tablespoons of oil and mix to a soft dough. Knead until smooth, adding more flour if the dough is sticky, or more water if it is dry.

2 Wrap in clingfilm and rest the pastry for 30 minutes. Meanwhile, mix all the filling ingredients together in a large bowl.

3 Knead the dough again and roll into 16 balls. Roll out each one to a 7.5cm/3 inch circle and keep the dough covered with a damp cloth.

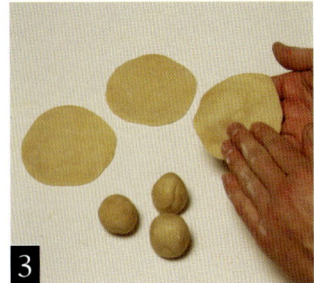

4 Place a teaspoon of filling on each pastry. Moisten the edges with water and fold each circle in half to make a semicircle. Pinch the edges together with thumb and forefinger to make a Cornish pasty shape, with a frilled seam on top and a flat base.

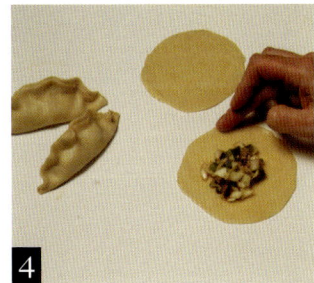

5 Heat 2 tablespoons of oil in a frying pan large enough to lie the dumplings in one layer. Fry the dumplings over a low heat until the flat bases are crisp and golden.

6 Pour over the stock and cover the pan with a tightly fitting lid or some foil. Simmer over a low heat for 8-10 minutes until the liquid has been absorbed and the dumplings are cooked through. Serve with chilli or plum dipping sauce.

# Chilli Sauce & Edible Garnishes

## Easy Entertaining

Chilli sauce is served with seafood or delicate foods such as dumplings for dipping.

### Sweet chilli sauce:

**50g/2oz caster sugar**
**50ml/2 fl oz rice vinegar**
**2 tbsp water**
**2 red chillies, finely chopped**

1 Heat the sugar and rice vinegar together in a heavy-based saucepan, with 2 tablespoons of water, stirring until the grains of sugar have dissolved.

2 Bring to the boil and keep boiling until a clear syrup forms. Remove from the heat and stir in the chillies. Cool completely before serving in small bowls for dipping.

Garnishes play a vital part in Chinese food as the way food is presented is very important. These pretty garnishes can be used to decorate most dishes.

# Spring Onion Tassels

Cut most of the green part away from the spring onion and trim the base of the bulb. Make lengthways cuts about 2.5cm/1 inch long into each end. Soak the spring onions in iced water, when the cut ends will curl up.

# Chilli Flowers

Trim the tip from a chilli, but do not remove the stem. Make 4 cuts lengthways from the stem of the chilli to the tip, to form 4 sections. Remove any seeds and chill in iced water when the 4 sections will curl up and spread out into flower shapes.

# Carrot Flowers

Peel a carrot and cut into 7.5cm/3 inch chunks. Make a shallow V-shaped cut down the length of each slice. Repeat, making 4 cuts lengthways around each carrot. Cut thinly crossways to make flower-shaped slices.

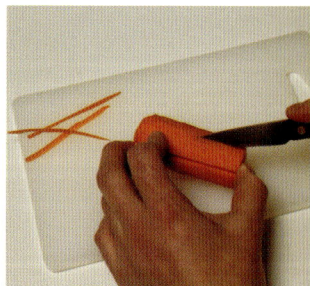

# fish
and
# seafood

# Ginger & Spring Onion Crab

*Easy Entertaining*

These delicious pieces of crab are much easier to eat with your fingers, so serve this dish with fingerbowls of warm water and a slice of lemon.

## Ingredients for 2

**2 medium-sized, cooked crabs**
**2 tbsp rice wine or dry sherry**
**2 tbsp sunflower oil**
**2.5cm/1 inch root ginger, peeled and finely chopped**
**4 spring onions, sliced**
**175g/6oz black bean sauce**
**2 tbsp vegetable or fish stock**

## Ingredients for 4

**4 medium-sized, cooked crabs**
**4 tbsp rice wine or dry sherry**
**4 tbsp sunflower oil**
**5cm/2 inch root ginger, peeled and finely chopped**
**8 spring onions, sliced**
**350g/12oz black bean sauce**
**4 tbsp vegetable or fish stock**

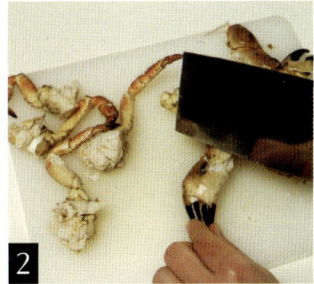

1 Wash the crabs well. Lift the main shell by levering with a knife, and remove the feathery gills and sac and discard.

2 Chop the body into 4-6 pieces, each piece with one of the legs attached. Crack the shell with a cleaver or heavy knife. Sprinkle over the wine or sherry and chill for 30 minutes.

3 Heat the oil in a wok or large pan and fry the ginger and half the spring onions for 3 minutes to soften. Add the crab pieces and stir-fry for 2 minutes.

4 Add the black bean sauce and the stock and stir-fry for 4 minutes, turning the crabs over occasionally. Serve sprinkled with the remaining spring onions.

# Squid with Green Pepper

*Quick and Easy*

Squid takes only minutes to cook, but don't be tempted to over-cook it or it can become rubbery.

## Ingredients for 2

225g/8oz fresh squid
4 tbsp sunflower oil
1/2 green pepper, thinly sliced
2 cloves garlic, peeled and chopped
2.5cm/1 inch root ginger, peeled and sliced
50g/2oz beansprouts
1 tbsp light soy sauce
1 tsp rice vinegar
1 tbsp coriander, chopped

## Ingredients for 4

450g/1lb fresh squid
6 tbsp sunflower oil
1 green pepper, thinly sliced
2 cloves garlic, peeled and chopped
5cm/2 inch root ginger, peeled and sliced
100g/4oz beansprouts
2 tbsp light soy sauce
2 tsp rice vinegar
2 tbsp coriander, chopped

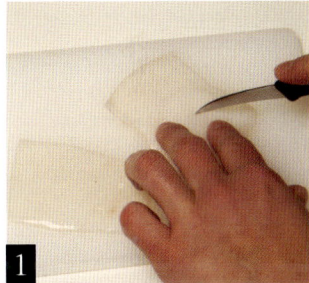

1 Clean the squid, remove the heads and ink sacs. Remove the quill and wash the body in water until it runs clear. Cut down the centre of the body lengthways. Flatten the squid out and score a lattice pattern into the flesh with a sharp knife. If the squid are large, cut into smaller oblongs.

2 Heat half the oil in a wok or large frying pan and stir-fry the squid quickly over a high heat for 1 minute, until the pieces curl up. Remove from the pan with a slotted spoon and drain on kitchen paper.

3 Add the remaining oil to the pan and stir-fry the pepper, garlic and ginger with the beansprouts for 4 minutes until softened.

4 Return the squid to the pan with the soy sauce and vinegar and cook over a high heat for 1 minute, stirring constantly. Serve sprinkled with chopped coriander.

# Sweet & Sour Prawns

*Quick and Easy*

Everyone loves sweet and sour dishes and this one, made all in one pan, couldn't be easier.

## Ingredients for 2

**225g/8oz raw peeled prawns**
**2 tsp sunflower oil**
**1 clove garlic, chopped**
**2.5cm/1 inch root ginger, peeled and chopped**
**2 spring onions, sliced**
**1/2 red pepper, seeded and diced**
**100g/4oz canned water chestnuts**

### Sauce:

**1/2 tbsp cornflour**
**5 tbsp chicken stock**
**1 tbsp rice wine or dry sherry**
**2 tbsp soy sauce**
**1 tbsp tomato puree**
**1 1/2 tbsp rice vinegar**
**1/2 tbsp caster sugar**

## Ingredients for 4

**450g/1lb raw peeled prawns**
**1 tbsp sunflower oil**
**1 clove garlic, chopped**
**5cm/2 inch root ginger, peeled and chopped**
**4 spring onions, sliced**
**1 red pepper, seeded and diced**
**225g/8oz canned water chestnuts**

### Sauce:

**1 tbsp cornflour**
**150ml/1/4 pint chicken stock**
**2 tbsp rice wine or dry sherry**
**4 tbsp soy sauce**
**2 tbsp tomato puree**
**3 tbsp rice vinegar**
**1 tbsp caster sugar**

1 Heat the oil in a wok or large frying pan and stir-fry the garlic, ginger and spring onions for 1 minute.

2 Add the pepper and stir fry for 1 minute, then add the prawns and stir-fry for 30 seconds until they turn pink.

3 Blend the cornflour to a paste with 2 tablespoons of cold water, then mix in a jug with all the sauce ingredients.

4 Stir well, then pour into the wok. Add the water chestnuts and cook over a medium heat for 4 minutes until the sauce has thickened and is piping hot. Serve with plain boiled rice.

# Kung Pao Prawns with Cashew Nuts

*One Pot*

This colourful dish is enriched with crunchy cashew nuts.

## Ingredients for 2

1 clove garlic, chopped
2.5cm/1 inch root ginger,
    peeled and chopped
1 tbsp cornflour
1/4 tsp bicarbonate of soda
225g/8oz peeled, uncooked
    prawns
2 tbsp sunflower oil
1 small onion, chopped
1 courgette, diced
1/2 red pepper, diced
25g/1oz cashew nuts

### Sauce:

90ml/3fl oz chicken stock
1 tsp chilli sauce
2 tbsp yellow bean paste
1/2 tbsp rice wine or dry
    sherry

## Ingredients for 4

1 clove garlic, chopped
5cm/2 inch root ginger,
    peeled and chopped
1 tbsp cornflour
1/4 tsp bicarbonate of soda
450g/1lb peeled, uncooked
    prawns
4 tbsp sunflower oil
1 medium onion, chopped
2 small courgettes, diced
1 red pepper, diced
50g/2oz cashew nuts

### Sauce:

175ml/6fl oz chicken stock
2 tsp chilli sauce
4 tbsp yellow bean paste
1 tbsp rice wine or dry
    sherry

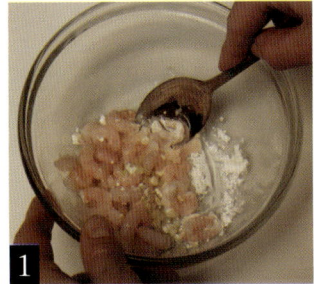

1 Mix the garlic, ginger, cornflour and bicarbonate of soda together and season with salt and pepper. Stir in the prawns and chill for 10 minutes.

2 Heat the oil in a wok or large frying pan, add the prawns and cook over a high heat for 30 seconds. Remove to a plate with a slotted spoon and keep warm.

3 Add the onion to the wok and cook for 1 minute. Add the courgettes and red pepper and cook for a further 2 minutes.

4 Mix the sauce ingredients together and add to the pan. Cook until hot and thickened, then add the prawns and cashew nuts and stir-fry to heat thoroughly. Serve with fried rice.

# Grilled Prawns with Fresh Coriander

*Low Fat*

Serve these hot, tangy prawns as a quick starter or a light lunch, with a salad and a noodle dish.

## Ingredients for 2

**225g/8oz raw prawns**

### Marinade:
**2 tsp light soy sauce**
**1 tsp rice wine or dry sherry**
**1 tsp sesame oil**

### Topping:
**1 tbsp fresh coriander**
**1 tsp rice vinegar**
**1 tsp root ginger, finely chopped**
**Lime wedges to serve**

## Ingredients for 4

**450g/1lb raw prawns**

### Marinade:
**1 tbsp light soy sauce**
**2 tsp rice wine or dry sherry**
**2 tsp sesame oil**

### Topping:
**2 tbsp fresh coriander**
**2 tsp rice vinegar**
**2 tsp root ginger, finely chopped**
**Lime wedges to serve**

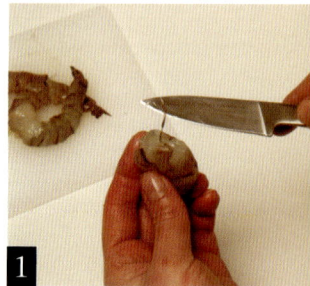

1 Peel to remove the heads, shells and legs from the prawns. Using a sharp knife, remove the black vein from the back of each prawn.

2 Mix the soy sauce, wine and sesame oil together. Toss the prawns in the mixture and chill for 15 minutes.

3 Preheat the grill to hot. Lay the prawns on the grill pan. Grill the prawns for two minutes. Turn them over and grill for another 2 minutes until they are cooked and turn pink.

4 Mix the coriander and ginger with the vinegar in a small bowl. Toss the prawns in the mixture then serve immediately.

# Spicy Salmon with Spring Onions

*Easy Entertaining*

This quick and easy dish makes an ideal main course for a supper party with friends.

## Ingredients for 2

**225g/8oz salmon fillets**
**1 tsp Sichuan peppercorns,**
    **freshly ground**
**1 tsp salt**
**300ml/¹/₂ pint fish stock**

### Topping:

**2 spring onions, thinly sliced**
**2.5cm/1 inch root ginger,**
    **peeled**
**2 tsp sunflower oil**
**1 tsp chilli or sesame oil**

## Ingredients for 4

**450g/1lb salmon fillets**
**2 Sichuan peppercorns,**
    **freshly ground**
**2 tsp salt**
**600ml/1 pint fish stock**

### Topping:

**4 spring onions, thinly sliced**
**5cm/2 inch root ginger,**
    **peeled**
**1 tbsp sunflower oil**
**2 tsp chilli or sesame oil**

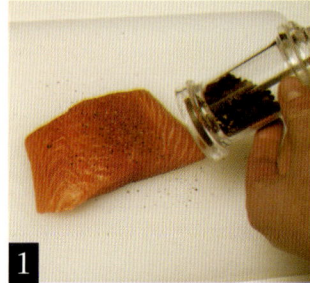

1 Sprinkle the salmon fillets with the pepper and half the salt. Place the fish in a single layer in a frying pan or roasting dish.

2 Heat the fish stock to boiling, then pour into the pan. Simmer for 3 minutes then cover the pan tightly with a lid, or foil, and turn off the heat.

3 Leave the salmon to stand for 6 minutes. Remove the cooked salmon from the stock and place on warmed serving plates. Scatter the sliced spring onions and ginger over the fish.

4 Heat the sunflower oil and sesame oil together until very hot, then pour over the topping. Serve immediately with plain boiled rice and steamed pak choi.

# Singapore Fish

*Hot and spicy*

The flavours of the East combine with those of China in this tasty dish.

## Ingredients for 2

**225g/8oz firm white fish fillets such as cod or haddock**
**½ large egg white**
**1 tbsp cornflour**
**1 tsp white wine**
**Salt and pepper**
**4 tbsp sunflower oil**
**1 small onion, sliced**
**½ tbsp mild curry powder**
**225g/8oz can pineapple pieces**
**100g/4oz frozen or canned water chestnuts, drained**
**½ tbsp lime juice**

## Ingredients for 4

**450g/1lb firm white fish fillets such as cod or haddock**
**1 large egg white**
**2 tbsp cornflour**
**2 tsp white wine**
**Salt and pepper**
**6 tbsp sunflower oil**
**1 large onion, sliced**
**1 tbsp mild curry powder**
**350g/12oz can pineapple pieces**
**225g/8oz frozen or canned water chestnuts, drained**
**1 tbsp lime juice**

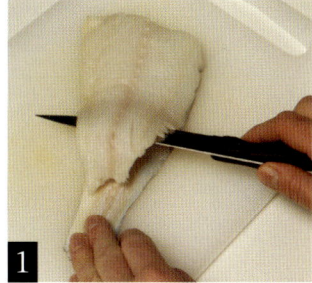

1 Remove the skin from the fillets with a sharp knife and cut the fish into 5cm/2 inch chunks. Mix the egg white with half the cornflour and the white wine and season with salt and pepper.

2 Dip the fish in the mixture and leave to stand for 5 minutes. Heat the oil in a wok or frying pan and fry the fish, a few pieces at a time. Drain on kitchen paper and keep warm.

3 Pour away all but 1 tablespoon oil from the pan and fry the onion for 3 minutes until softened. Add the curry powder and cook for 2 minutes. Add the juice from the pineapple can and 2-3 tablespoons of water if necessary.

4 Blend the remaining cornflour with the lime juice, add to the pan and boil until thickened. Add the pineapple pieces and water chestnuts, cook for 1 minute to heat, then pour over the fish on a serving platter.

# Five-spice Fish

## Quick and Easy

Enriched with the flavours of ginger and five-spice powder, ordinary white fish is turned into a feast.

### Ingredients for 2

**225g/8oz firm white fish fillets such as cod or haddock**
**1 tsp five- spice powder**
**1/2 tsp salt**
**1 tbsp sunflower oil**
**1 clove garlic, peeled and chopped**
**2.5cm/1 inch root ginger, peeled and chopped**
**2 tbsp rice wine or dry sherry**
**1 tsp soy sauce**
**1 tsp sesame oil**
**Fresh coriander leaves**

### Ingredients for 4

**450g/1lb firm white fish fillets such as cod or haddock**
**2 tsp five-spice powder**
**1 tsp salt**
**2 tbsp sunflower oil**
**2 cloves garlic, peeled and chopped**
**5cm/2 inch root ginger, peeled and chopped**
**4 tbsp rice wine or dry sherry**
**2 tsp soy sauce**
**2 tsp sesame oil**
**Fresh coriander leaves**

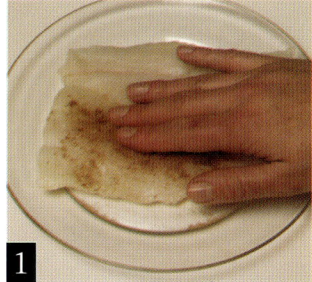

1 Rub the fish fillets with the five-spice powder and sprinkle with salt.

2 Heat the oil in a wok or large frying pan and shallow-fry the fillets for 5 minutes until golden brown, turning over once during the cooking.

3 Remove the fish from the pan and keep warm. Add the garlic and ginger to the pan and cook for 2 minutes to soften.

4 Sprinkle over the rice wine, soy sauce and sesame oil and cook for a minute. Add the fish and cook for 30 seconds to heat through. Serve with vegetables and fresh coriander.

# Sichuan Scallops

Low Fat

Scallops are sweet and delicate and ideal for stir-frying. Do watch the timing and don't over-cook them, as they will become tough.

## Ingredients for 2

**1 tbsp sunflower oil**
**2.5cm/1 inch root ginger,** chopped
**2 spring onions, finely** chopped
**175g/6oz fresh whole** scallops with corals

### Sauce:

**2 tsp rice wine or dry** sherry
**1 tsp light soy sauce**
**1 tsp chilli sauce**
**1 tsp tomato puree**
**1/2 tsp caster sugar**
**1/2 tsp sesame oil**

## Ingredients for 4

**2 tbsp sunflower oil**
**2.5cm/1 inch root ginger,** chopped
**4 spring onions, finely** chopped
**350g/12oz fresh whole** scallops with corals

### Sauce:

**1 tbsp rice wine or dry** sherry
**2 tsp light soy sauce**
**2 tsp chilli sauce**
**2 tsp tomato puree**
**1 tsp caster sugar**
**1 tsp sesame oil**

1 Heat the oil in a wok or a large frying pan and add the ginger and spring onions. Stir-fry for 1 minute until softened.

2 Add the scallops and stir-fry for 30 seconds.

3 Add all the sauce ingredients except the sesame oil and cook for 3 minutes until the scallops are slightly firm.

4 Sprinkle over the sesame oil, stir-fry for 30 seconds and serve immediately.

# Prawn Fu Yung

*One Pan*

This tasty dish makes an ideal quick midweek dinner.

## Ingredients for 2

1 tbsp sunflower oil
1 carrot, cut into fine
  matchsticks
1 spring onion, sliced
25g/1oz frozen peas,
  blanched
2 large eggs, beaten
2 tsp light soy sauce
100g/4oz frozen cooked
  prawns, thawed
2 tsp sesame seeds
1 tsp sesame oil

## Ingredients for 4

2 tbsp sunflower oil
2 carrots, cut into fine
  matchsticks
2 spring onions, sliced
50g/2oz frozen peas,
  blanched
4 large eggs, beaten
1 tbsp light soy sauce
225g/8oz frozen cooked
  prawns, thawed
4 tsp sesame seeds
2 tsp sesame oil

1 Heat the oil in a wok or a large frying pan. Stir-fry the carrot and spring onions for 2 minutes, then remove to a plate with a slotted spoon and keep warm. Beat the eggs lightly with the soy sauce until smooth.

2 Add the eggs to the wok and cook, stirring gently to break the eggs up, for 2 minutes.

3 Add the carrot , spring onions and peas and cook for 1 minute. Add the prawns and cook for just 30 seconds to heat the prawns.

4 Turn out onto serving plates and serve sprinkled with sesame seeds and oil.

# chicken and duck

# Braised Chicken Casserole

One Pot

This dish contains salted black bean sauce which adds a spicy richness to chicken dishes.

## Ingredients for 2

**2 tsp sunflower oil**
**450g/1lb chicken thigh joints**
**1 clove garlic**
**2cm/³/₄ inch root ginger**
**¹/₂ an orange**
**¹/₂ red chilli**
**2 tbsp black bean sauce**
**1 tsp light soy sauce**

## Ingredients for 4

**1 tbsp sunflower oil**
**900g/2lb chicken thigh joints**
**2 cloves garlic**
**2.5cm/1 inch root ginger**
**1 orange**
**1 red chilli**
**4 tbsp black bean sauce**
**2 tsp light soy sauce**

1 Remove the skin from the chicken joints. Peel and finely chop the garlic and ginger. Remove the seeds from the chilli and chop finely.

2 Heat the oil in a deep, heavy-based saucepan or wok. Add the chicken joints and brown them all over. Add the chopped garlic, ginger and chilli and stir-fry for 1 minute.

3 Cut long strips of rind from the orange with a potato peeler, then cut into thin slivers. Squeeze the juice from the orange.

4 Add the orange juice and rind, black beans and soy sauce and bring to the boil. Lower the heat and simmer, covered, for 20-30 minutes until the chicken is tender. Add 2-3 tablespoons of water if the dish dries out. Serve with a noodle dish.

# Chicken with Peanuts

*Hot and spicy*

You can also make this dish with cashew nuts to add an extra taste of luxury.

## Ingredients for 2

1 tbsp peanut or sunflower oil
50g/2oz fresh peanuts,
    shelled and skinned
1 small red chilli, seeded and
    sliced
100g/4oz chicken breasts,
    skinned, boned and cubed
1 small green pepper, seeded
    and sliced

### Sauce:

90ml/3 fl oz chicken stock
1 tsp rice wine or dry sherry
1 tsp dark soy sauce
1/2 tsp sugar
1 tsp root ginger, finely
    chopped
1 clove garlic, peeled and
    chopped
1 spring onion, chopped

## Ingredients for 4

1 tbsp peanut or sunflower
    oil
100g/4oz fresh peanuts,
    shelled and skinned
1 red chilli, seeded and sliced
225g/8oz chicken breasts,
    skinned, boned and cubed
1 green pepper, seeded and
    sliced

### Sauce:

150ml/1/4 pint chicken stock
1 tbsp rice wine or dry sherry
1 tbsp dark soy sauce
1 tsp sugar
1 tsp root ginger, finely
    chopped
1 clove garlic, peeled and
    chopped
2 spring onions, chopped

1 Heat the oil in a wok or large frying pan and stir-fry the peanuts for a few seconds. Remove from the pan with a slotted spoon. Add the chilli and chicken to the pan and stir-fry for 2 minutes.

2 Add the pepper and stir-fry for a further 2 minutes. Remove from the pan with a slotted spoon.

3 Add all the sauce ingredients to the wok and bring to the boil. Simmer for 5 minutes.

4 Add the chicken and peanuts to the pan with the sauce and cook for 2 minutes until piping hot. Serve with plain or fried rice.

# Barbecued Chicken

*Family Favourite*

This chicken is perfect for cooking outside in the summer on the barbecue. It's also great as a cold dish for lunch boxes.

## Ingredients for 2

1 tsp five-spice powder
2 tbsp hoisin sauce
1 tbsp clear honey
1 tbsp tomato ketchup
450g/1lb chicken
    drumsticks
100g/4oz egg noodles
1 red pepper, seeded and
    chopped
1 tbsp sesame oil

## Ingredients for 4

2 tsp five-spice powder
4 tbsp hoisin sauce
2 tbsp clear honey
2 tbsp tomato ketchup
800g/1¾lb chicken
    drumsticks
250g/9oz egg noodles
2 red peppers, seeded and
    chopped
2 tbsp sesame oil

1 Preheat the oven to 220°C/425°F/Gas 7. Mix the five-spice powder, hoisin sauce, tomato ketchup and honey together.

2 Prick the drumsticks all over with a fork and place in a shallow bowl. Brush the marinade over the drumsticks to coat them.

3 Place the chicken in an oiled ovenproof dish and bake for 20 minutes or until tender, basting occasionally.

4 Make the noodle salad. Cook the noodles in boiling water, according to the instructions on the packet and drain. Heat the sesame oil in a wok and stir-fry the peppers for 2 minutes. Add the cooked noodles and stir together. Serve immediately with the chicken legs.

# Lemon Chicken

*Quick and Easy*

You may be surprised to find custard powder as an ingredient for this recipe, but it is commonly used in Chinese restaurants to create savoury sauces.

## Ingredients for 2

**225g/8oz chicken breasts, skinned and boned**
**2 tsp cornflour**
**1 tbsp sunflower oil**
**1 tbsp custard powder**
**2 tbsp lemon juice**
**2 tsp soft light brown sugar**
**1 tbsp rice wine or dry sherry**
**1 tsp light soy sauce**
**150ml/1/4 pint chicken stock**
**1 spring onion, cut into curls**

## Ingredients for 4

**450g/1lb chicken breasts, skinned and boned**
**4 tsp cornflour**
**2 tbsp sunflower oil**
**2 tbsp custard powder**
**4 tbsp lemon juice**
**1 tbsp soft light brown sugar**
**2 tbsp rice wine or dry sherry**
**2 tsp light soy sauce**
**300ml/1/2 pint chicken stock**
**2 spring onions, cut into curls**

1 Place the custard powder in a jug and mix to a paste with 3 tablespoons of water. Add the lemon juice, sugar wine, and soy sauce, stir together then pour into a saucepan. Add the chicken stock and heat gently until the mixture thickens, stirring constantly. Turn off the heat.

2 Cut the chicken breasts into 2.5cm/1 inch chunks. Dust lightly in the cornflour to coat the pieces.

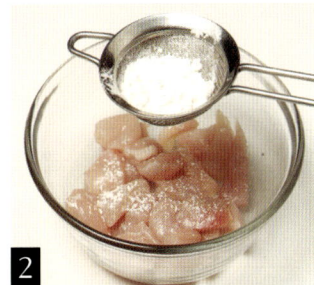

3 Heat the oil in a large frying pan or wok and stir-fry the chicken for 10 minutes until crisp and golden. If you do not have a large pan, fry the chicken in batches.

4 Place the chicken on a warmed serving dish. Reheat the sauce until bubbling, then pour over the chicken and serve immediately. Decorate with spring onion curls.

# Drunken Chicken

*Easy Entertaining*

Make this dish well ahead of time to allow the chicken to absorb the flavour of the rice wine.

## Ingredients for 2

**175g/6oz whole chicken
     breasts, skinned and
     boned**
**1 thick slice root ginger,
     peeled**
**1 stick celery, thinly sliced**
**1 tbsp soft light brown sugar**
**Pinch of salt**
**70ml/2¹/₂fl oz chicken stock**
**70ml/2¹/₂fl oz yellow rice wine
     or sweet sherry**

## Ingredients for 4

**350g/12oz whole chicken
     breasts, skinned and
     boned**
**2 thick slices root ginger,
     peeled**
**2 sticks celery, thinly sliced**
**1 tbsp soft light brown sugar**
**¹/₂ tsp salt**
**150ml/¹/₄ pint chicken stock**
**150ml/¹/₄ pint yellow rice
     wine or sweet sherry**

1 Place the chicken breasts in a deep saucepan and add the ginger, celery, sugar and salt.

2 Pour the chicken stock over the chicken to cover it, and bring to the boil. Cover and simmer for 20-30 minutes until the chicken is tender.

3 Turn off the heat and add the rice wine or sherry. Leave the chicken to cool completely in the liquid for 1 hour.

4 Remove the chicken from the pan, place on a chopping board and cut into thick diagonal slices. Place the chicken in a plastic container and strain the cooking liquid over through a sieve. Chill for 12 hours, turning the chicken over in the liquid occasionally. Serve the sliced chicken cold with a warm salad.

# Chinese Chicken Curry

*One Pot*

Chinese curries are not as hot as Indian ones, and have a sweeter, spicier flavour.

## Ingredients for 2

- 1/2 tbsp medium curry paste
- 1 tsp five-spice powder
- 1/2 tbsp cornflour
- 1 tbsp sunflower oil
- 1 medium onion, peeled and chopped
- 1/2 green and 1/2 red pepper, seeded and sliced
- 225g/8oz chicken breast, skinned, boned and cubed
- 1 tsp sugar
- 1 tbsp tomato ketchup
- 5 tbsp chicken stock

## Ingredients for 4

- 1 tbsp medium curry paste
- 1 tsp five-spice powder
- 1 tbsp cornflour
- 2 tbsp sunflower oil
- 1 large onion, peeled and chopped
- 1 green and 1 red pepper, seeded and sliced
- 450g/1lb chicken breast, skinned, boned and cubed
- 1 tsp sugar
- 1 tbsp tomato ketchup
- 150ml/1/4 pint chicken stock

1 Mix the curry paste and the five-spice powder together. Blend the cornflour to a paste with 2 tablespoons of water.

2 Heat the oil in a large wok or frying pan and fry the onion for 2 minutes to soften it. Add the peppers and stir-fry for 2 minutes.

3 Add the cubed chicken and fry to brown for 5 minutes. Add the curry paste and stir-fry for 2 minutes, coating the chicken in the pan.

4 Add the sugar, ketchup and stock with the cornflour paste. Bring to the boil then simmer, stirring occasionally for 15-20 minutes. Serve piping hot with rice.

# Hot and Spicy Stir-fry

*Quick and Easy*

Stir-fry oil is a ready-flavoured, blended oil with garlic, ginger and chilli. If you cannot find it, use one-third sunflower oil, one-third sesame oil, and one-third chilli oil instead.

## Ingredients for 2

2 tbsp hoisin sauce
1 tbsp red bean paste
1 tsp chilli and garlic sauce
1 tsp light soy sauce
1 tsp sugar
1 tsp rice wine vinegar
225g/8oz chicken breasts,
    skinned and boned
1 tbsp stir-fry oil
75g/3oz mangetout

## Ingredients for 4

4 tbsp hoisin sauce
1 tbsp red bean paste
1 tbsp chilli and garlic sauce
1 tbsp light soy sauce
1 tbsp sugar
1 tbsp rice wine vinegar
450g/1lb chicken breasts,
    skinned and boned
2 tbsp stir-fry oil
150g/5oz mangetout

1 Mix the hoisin sauce, red bean paste, chilli and garlic sauce, soy sauce, sugar and vinegar together.

2 Cut the chicken into thin strips and coat in the paste. Allow to marinate in the refrigerator for 15 minutes or longer.

3 Heat the stir-fry oil in a wok or large frying pan. Stir-fry the chicken strips for 3-4 minutes until browned.

4 Add the mangetout and cook for 3 minutes until tender. Serve immediately with freshly cooked noodles.

# Fried Chicken Livers with Ginger

Low Fat

Chicken livers are inexpensive and very quick to cook, so you can make this dish in minutes.

## Ingredients for 2

225g/8oz chicken livers,
   thawed if frozen
15g/¹/₂ oz cornflour
1 tbsp stir-fry oil
1 clove garlic, finely chopped
1 spring onion, finely
   chopped
1 tsp sesame oil
50g/2oz brown cap
   mushrooms, sliced
2.5cm/1 inch root ginger,
   peeled and finely grated
2 tsp dark soy sauce
2 tsp lemon juice
Fresh coriander and finely
   sliced lemon rind strips
   to serve

## Ingredients for 4

350g/12oz chicken livers,
   thawed if frozen
25g/1oz cornflour
2 tbsp stir-fry oil
2 cloves garlic, finely chopped
2 spring onions, finely
   chopped
1 tsp sesame oil
100g/4oz brown cap
   mushrooms, sliced
2.5cm/1 inch root ginger,
   peeled and finely grated
1 tbsp dark soy sauce
1 tbsp lemon juice
Fresh coriander and finely
   sliced lemon rind strips
   to serve

1 Clean the livers and remove any membranes. Pat them dry on kitchen paper. Dust lightly in the cornflour.

2 Heat half the stir-fry oil in a wok or deep frying pan and stir-fry the livers for 1-2 minutes until golden. Remove to a plate with a slotted spoon and keep warm.

3 Heat the remaining oil with the sesame oil and stir-fry the garlic, ginger, spring onions and sliced mushrooms for 2 minutes to soften.

4 Return the chicken livers to the pan, add the soy sauce and lemon juice and stir-fry for 2 minutes until sizzling hot. Serve immediately scattered with coriander and thinly sliced lemon rind strips.

# Crispy Chicken in Yellow Bean Sauce

*Quick and Easy*

Yellow bean sauce is a favourite in Chinese food stores, but you will find it readily available from most supermarkets.

## Ingredients for 2

**225g/8oz chicken breasts,**
**skinned, boned**
**1/2 egg white**
**1/2 tbsp cornflour**
**1 tbsp sunflower oil**
**1 clove garlic, chopped**
**1 small green pepper, diced**
**25g/1oz baby corn cobs**
**1/2 tbsp rice wine vinegar**
**1 tbsp light soy sauce**
**1/2 tsp sugar**
**3 tbsp yellow bean sauce**

## Ingredients for 4

**450g/1lb chicken breasts,**
**skinned, boned**
**1 egg white**
**1 tbsp cornflour**
**2 tbsp sunflower oil**
**1 clove garlic, chopped**
**1 green pepper, diced**
**50g/2oz baby corn cobs**
**1 tbsp rice wine vinegar**
**1 tbsp light soy sauce**
**1/2 tsp sugar**
**4 tbsp yellow bean sauce**

1 Cut the chicken into 2.5cm/1 inch cubes. Whisk the egg white with the cornflour, add the cubed chicken and coat it well.

2 Heat half the oil in a wok and stir-fry the chicken for about 4 minutes until crisp and golden. Remove from the pan with a slotted spoon and keep warm on a plate lined with kitchen paper.

3 Add the remaining oil to the wok and stir-fry the garlic, pepper and corn cobs for 2-3 minutes.

4 Add the vinegar, soy sauce, sugar and yellow bean sauce to the pan and cook for 1-2 minutes, stirring until hot. Serve on a platter with the chicken pieces on top.

# Stir-fried Duck with Broccoli

*One Pan*

The delicate vegetables and ginger strips in this stir-fry make a fresh contrast with the richness of the duck breasts.

## Ingredients for 2

- 1 duck breast, 175g/6oz
- 2 tsp rice wine
- 2 tsp dark soy sauce
- 1 tbsp sunflower oil
- 1 clove garlic, crushed
- 2.5cm/1 inch root ginger, peeled
- 1 spring onion
- 50g/2oz broccoli
- 75g/3oz beansprouts
- 2 tbsp oyster sauce

## Ingredients for 4

- 2 duck breasts 175g/6oz each
- 1 tbsp rice wine
- 1 tbsp dark soy sauce
- 2 tbsp sunflower oil
- 1 clove garlic, crushed
- 5cm/2 inch root ginger, peeled
- 2 spring onions
- 100g/4oz broccoli
- 175g/6oz beansprouts
- 4 tbsp oyster sauce

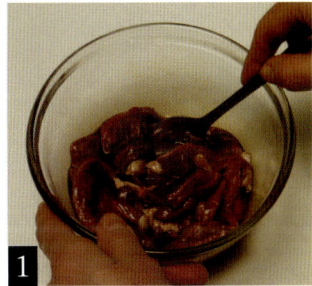

1 Cut the duck breast into thin strips and place in a bowl with the rice wine and soy sauce. Stir to coat, then chill in the refrigerator for 30 minutes.

2 Cut the ginger and spring onions into thin matchstick slivers. Separate the broccoli into florets and cut in half if they are too large.

3 Heat the oil in a wok or a deep frying pan and stir-fry the duck for 3 minutes until browned all over. Remove to a plate and keep warm.

4 Stir-fry the garlic, ginger and onions for 2 minutes, add the broccoli and beansprouts and stir-fry again for 2-3 minutes until the vegetables begin to soften. Add the duck and the oyster sauce and cook for 2 minutes until piping hot. Serve immediately with noodles.

# beef
*and*
# lamb

# Beef in Oyster Sauce

*Easy Entertaining*

This sliced-beef dish has a mellow flavour and makes a good contrast when served with hot and fiery dishes.

## Ingredients for 2

**225g/8oz rump steak**
**2 tsp dark soy sauce**
**1 tsp sesame oil**
**2 tsp rice wine or dry sherry**
**1 tsp cornflour**
**1 tbsp sunflower oil**
**50g/2oz oyster mushrooms**
**2 tbsp oyster sauce**
**½ small leek, cleaned and finely shredded**

## Ingredients for 4

**450g/1lb rump steak**
**1 tbsp dark soy sauce**
**2 tsp sesame oil**
**1 tbsp rice wine or dry sherry**
**2 tsp cornflour**
**2 tbsp sunflower oil**
**100g/4oz oyster mushrooms**
**4 tbsp oyster sauce**
**1 small leek, cleaned and finely shredded**

1 Cut the steak into thin slices 5cm/2 inches long across the grain of the meat, using a cleaver or a large, sharp knife.

2 Mix the soy sauce, sesame oil, wine or sherry and cornflour together and spread over the meat. Leave to marinate for 30 minutes or longer.

3 Heat the oil in a wok or large frying pan and stir-fry the beef strips for 3 minutes until the beef is browned all over. Add the mushrooms and cook for 1 minute until wilted.

4 Add the oyster sauce to the pan and stir-fry until the beef is hot and bubbling. Serve scattered with fine leek shreds. Accompany with a noodle dish.

# Stir-fried Beef with Ginger

*Hot and spicy*

This dry stir-fry is fiery and makes a great contrast to blander dishes.

## Ingredients for 2

**175g/6oz lean beef steak,**
   **such as rump**
**2 tsp hoisin sauce**
**1/2 tsp five-spice powder**
**1 clove garlic, chopped**
**1 tsp sesame oil**
**2.5cm/1 inch root ginger,**
   **peeled and sliced**
**2 green chillies, chopped**
**1/2 red pepper, diced**
**3 spring onions, diced**
**25g/1oz canned sliced**
   **bamboo shoots, drained**

## Ingredients for 4

**350g/12oz lean beef steak,**
   **such as rump**
**1 tbsp hoisin sauce**
**1 tsp five-spice powder**
**2 cloves garlic, chopped**
**2 tsp sesame oil**
**5cm/2 inch root ginger,**
   **peeled and sliced**
**4 green chillies, chopped**
**1 red pepper, diced**
**6 spring onions, diced**
**50g/2oz canned sliced**
   **bamboo shoots, drained**

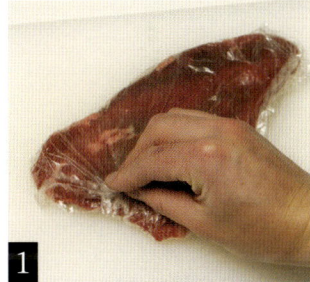

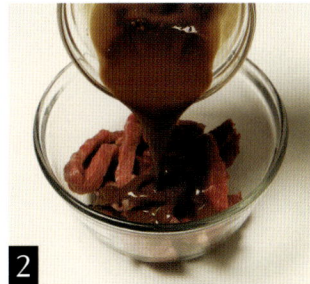

1 Wrap the steak in clingfilm and place in the freezer for 10 minutes, to make it firm for cutting. Cut the steak into thin slices 3.5cm/1¹/₂ inches long.

2 Mix the hoisin sauce, five-spice and garlic together, spread over the meat and marinate in the refrigerator for 1 hour or longer.

3 Heat the oil in a wok or large frying pan and stir-fry the ginger and chillies for 2 minutes.

4 Add the marinated beef to the pan and stir-fry for 2-3 minutes until the beef is browned and sizzling. Add the peppers, spring onions and bamboo shoots to the pan and stir-fry for 1 minute to heat, then serve immediately with rice or noodles.

# Steamed Beef Meatballs

*Family Favourite*

Prepare these meatballs ahead and steam them while you prepare other dishes such as stir-fries.

## Ingredients for 2

**225g/8oz lean minced beef**
**½ egg, beaten**
**½ tsp Sichuan peppercorns,**
  **freshly ground**
**1 tsp dark soy sauce**
**½ tsp sesame oil**
**1 tbsp coriander, chopped**
**2 spring onions, chopped**
**1 tsp cornflour**
**½ tsp sugar**
**2 tsp sunflower oil**
**½ leek, sliced**
**100g/4oz pak choi**

## Ingredients for 4

**450g/1lb lean minced beef**
**1 egg white**
**1 tsp Sichuan peppercorns,**
  **freshly ground**
**1 tbsp dark soy sauce**
**1 tsp sesame oil**
**2 tbsp coriander, chopped**
**4 spring onions, chopped**
**2 tsp cornflour**
**1 tsp sugar**
**1 tbsp sunflower oil**
**1 leek, sliced**
**225g/8oz pak choi**

1 Place the beef, egg white, pepper, soy sauce, sesame oil, coriander, spring onions, cornflour and sugar in a bowl and mix together.

2 Using wetted hands, make the paste into balls the size of golf balls. Put the meatballs on a plate and place in a steamer, or put them on a steaming rack over a wok full of hot water.

3 Cover and steam for 30 minutes, then keep warm. Heat the oil in a wok or pan and stir-fry the leek for 2 minutes to soften.

4 Separate the pak choi into leaves and add to the pan. Stir-fry for 2 minutes until wilted. Serve with the meatballs and plain rice.

# Stewed Beef

One Pot

This slowly cooked beef dish can be made ahead of time, cooled and stored in the fridge. Reheat thoroughly just before serving.

## Ingredients for 2

350g/12oz stewing beef
2 tsp sunflower oil
1 small onion, sliced
1 clove garlic, chopped
300ml/1/2 pint beef stock
1 tbsp dark soy sauce
2 tsp five-spice paste or
    powder
2 tbsp hoisin sauce
100g/4oz mooli

## Ingredients for 4

700g/11/2 lb stewing beef
1 tbsp sunflower oil
1 large onion, sliced
2 cloves garlic, chopped
600ml/1 pint beef stock
2 tbsp dark soy sauce
1 tbsp five-spice paste or
    powder
4 tbsp hoisin sauce
225g/8oz mooli

1 Trim the meat and cut into 2.5cm/1 inch cubes. Heat the oil in a wok or large frying pan and brown the beef. Add the onion and garlic and fry for 2 minutes.

2 Place the fried meat and onions in a deep heavy-based saucepan or heatproof casserole dish. Add all the remaining ingredients, except the mooli.

3 Bring to the boil, then turn down to a simmer. Either cook over a low heat, covered with a lid or piece of foil, for 11/2 hours, or bake in a preheated oven at 180°C/ 350°F/Gas 4 for 11/2 hours.

4 Peel the mooli and cut into 2.5cm/1 inch chunks or slices. Add to the pot and cook for a further 30 minutes until the meat is tender and falls apart. Serve immediately with large flat noodles, or cool and reheat later.

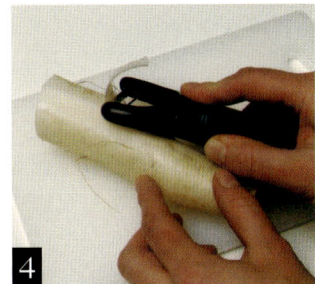

# Braised Lamb with Star Anise

*One Pot*

Star anise are whole spices shaped like little stars, with an aniseed flavour.

## Ingredients for 2

450g/1lb shoulder of lamb, boned
1 tbsp sunflower oil
1/2 leek, washed and sliced
2.5cm/1 inch root ginger, peeled
450ml/3/4 pint lamb stock
2 whole star anise
1 cinnamon stick
2 tbsp clear honey
1 tbsp rice wine or dry sherry
1 tbsp sesame paste
1 tbsp hoisin sauce
10g/4oz Chinese leaf

## Ingredients for 4

900g/2lb shoulder of lamb, boned
2 tbsp sunflower oil
1 leek, washed and sliced
5cm/2 inch root ginger, peeled
750ml/11/4 pint lamb stock
4 whole star anise
2 cinnamon sticks
3 tbsp clear honey
2 tbsp rice wine or dry sherry
2 tbsp sesame paste
2 tbsp hoisin sauce
225g/8oz Chinese leaf

1 Preheat the oven to 180°C/350°F/Gas 4. Cut the meat into 2.5cm/1 inch cubes. Heat the oil in a wok or large frying pan and stir-fry the meat in batches to brown. Place the meat in a heatproof casserole dish.

2 Add the leeks to the pan and stir-fry for 2 minutes to soften. Add the remaining ingredients except the Chinese leaf, and bring to the boil.

3 Pour the contents of the wok over the lamb in the casserole, cover and cook for 1 1/2 hours until tender. Alternatively, bake in a preheated oven at 180°C/ 350°F/Gas 4 for 1 1/2 hours.

4 Shred the Chinese leaf thickly and add to the pot. Cook for a further 15 minutes then serve with rice.

# Chilli Minced Lamb

*Quick and Easy*

This quick stir-fry makes a great midweek supper. Serve it with rice or noodles and pickled vegetables.

## Ingredients for 2

**1 tbsp sunflower oil**
**1 clove garlic, chopped**
**1 red chilli, seeded and finely chopped**
**2.5cm/1 inch root ginger, peeled and grated**
**225g/8oz lean minced lamb**
**2 tbsp tomato puree**
**1 tsp rice wine vinegar**
**1 tbsp dark soy sauce**
**1 tbsp rice wine or dry sherry**
**Fresh coriander to serve**

## Ingredients for 4

**2 tbsp sunflower oil**
**2 cloves garlic, chopped**
**2 red chillies, seeded and finely chopped**
**5cm/2 inch root ginger, peeled and grated**
**450g/1lb lean minced lamb**
**4 tbsp tomato puree**
**2 tsp rice wine vinegar**
**2 tbsp dark soy sauce**
**2 tbsp rice wine or dry sherry**
**Fresh coriander to serve**

1 Heat the oil in a wok or a large frying pan. Add the garlic, chilli and ginger and stir-fry for 2 minutes.

2 Add the minced lamb and stir-fry for 5 minutes until browned. Add the tomato puree, vinegar, soy sauce and rice wine or sherry.

3 Add 4-6 tablespoons of water and cover the pan. Cook over a simmering heat for 15 minutes.

4 Serve the lamb with flat egg noodles or rice and sprinkle with fresh coriander.

# Beef with Broccoli

*Easy Entertaining*

Part-freezing the meat for this dish makes it easy to cut into thin strips which will be tender and cook quickly.

## Ingredients for 2

225g/8oz rump steak
2 tbsp dark soy sauce
1 tbsp rice wine or dry
   sherry
½ tsp sugar
2 tsp cornflour
100g/4oz broccoli
50g/2oz carrots
2.5cm/1 inch root ginger,
   peeled and grated
1 tbsp sunflower oil

## Ingredients for 4

450g/1lb rump steak
4 tbsp dark soy sauce
2 tbsp rice wine or dry
   sherry
1 tsp sugar
1 tbsp cornflour
225g/8oz broccoli
100g/4oz carrots
2.5cm/1 inch root ginger,
   peeled and grated
2 tbsp sunflower oil

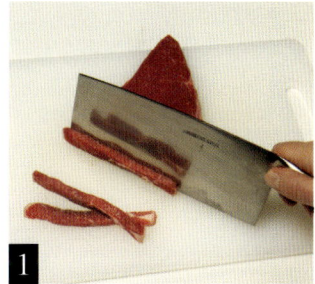

1 Place the steak in the freezer for 20 minutes to partially freeze. Remove from the freezer and cut into very thin slices across the grain of the meat.

2 Mix the soy sauce, rice wine, sugar and cornflour together and add the meat slices. Turn to coat the meat and leave to marinate for 30 minutes.

3 Trim the florets from the broccoli, cut into evenly sized pieces and slice any thick stalks. Cut the carrots into

matchsticks. Heat half the oil in a wok or large pan and stir fry the broccoli and carrots for 3-4 minutes to soften. Remove from the pan and keep warm.

4 Heat the remaining oil and add the ginger and the meat. Stir-fry for 2-3 minutes stirring constantly. Return the vegetables to the pan with any marinade from the dish and stir-fry for 1 minute to heat through. Serve immediately with fried rice.

# Chinese Pancakes with Beef

*Quick and Easy*

You can rustle up this dish in minutes, making it an ideal light lunch or supper for those in a hurry.

## Ingredients for 2

**4 Chinese pancakes (see page 68)**
**175g/6oz sirloin steak**
**1 tbsp sunflower oil**
**100g/4oz shitake mushrooms, sliced**
**225g/8oz pack stir-fried vegetables**
**75g/3oz black bean sauce**
**2 spring onions, thinly sliced**
**Fresh coriander and chilli sauce to garnish**

## Ingredients for 4

**8 Chinese pancakes (see page 68)**
**350g/12oz sirloin steak**
**2 tbsp sunflower oil**
**225g/8oz shitake mushrooms, sliced**
**350g/12oz pack stir-fried vegetables**
**175g/6oz black bean sauce**
**4 spring onions, thinly sliced**
**Fresh coriander and chilli sauce to garnish**

1 Place the pancakes on a steaming rack, in a steamer on a plate, or in the microwave to heat.

2 Cut the steak into very thin strips. Heat the oil in a wok or frying pan and fry the steak to brown all over for 1-2 minutes.

3 Add the vegetables and stir-fry for 3 minutes to soften. Stir in the black bean sauce and stir-fry for 1 minute.

4 Divide the stir-fry between the pancakes. Place the mixture on one half of each pancake and fold over the filling. Serve garnished with spring onions and fresh coriander. Drizzle with chilli sauce.

# Braised Lamb Chops

*Quick and Easy*

Try making this dish with pork chops instead of lamb.

## Ingredients for 2

**225g/8oz lamb chops**
**1cm/¹/₂ inch root ginger,**
  **peeled**
**2 spring onions**
**1 stick celery**
**2 tsp sunflower oil**
**1 tbsp rice wine or dry**
  **sherry**
**1 tbsp dark soy sauce**
**¹/₂ tsp sugar**
**50g/2oz pak choi or fresh**
  **spinach leaves**

## Ingredients for 4

**450g/1lb lamb chops**
**2.5cm/1 inch root ginger,**
  **peeled**
**4 spring onions**
**2 sticks celery**
**1 tbsp sunflower oil**
**2 tbsp rice wine or dry**
  **sherry**
**2 tbsp dark soy sauce**
**1 tsp sugar**
**100g/4oz pak choi or fresh**
  **spinach leaves**

1 Trim any excess fat from the lamb chops. Cut the ginger, spring onions and celery into fine shreds.

2 Heat the oil in a wok or large frying pan and fry the chops on both sides for 1-2 minutes to brown.

3 Add the sliced ginger, celery and onions and stir-fry for 1 minute, then add the rice wine and soy sauce with 3 tablespoons of water.

4 Cover and simmer for 5 minutes until the chops are tender. Separate and rinse the leaves and add to the pan. Cook for 1-2 minutes until wilted. Serve with boiled rice and a mixed vegetable dish.

# Sizzling Beef

*Easy Entertaining*

Celeriac stir-fries into delicate, golden, celery-flavoured straws which are deliciously crunchy with beef dishes.

## Ingredients for 2

**175g/6oz celeriac**
**3 spring onions**
**1 clove garlic, chopped**
**1 small pepper**
**2 tbsp sunflower oil**
**225g/8oz rump steak**
**3 tbsp beef stock**
**2 tsp dark soy sauce**
**2 tsp tomato puree**

## Ingredients for 4

**350g/12oz celeriac**
**6 spring onions**
**1 clove garlic, chopped**
**1 or 2 pepper**
**3 tbsp sunflower oil**
**450g/1lb rump steak**
**6 tbsp beef stock**
**1 tbsp dark soy sauce**
**1 tbsp tomato puree**

1 Peel the celeriac and cut into thin matchstick strips. Cut the spring onions and pepper into diamond shapes. Cut the steak into thin strips using a diagonal cut across the grain of the meat.

2 Heat half the oil in a wok or a deep pan. Stir-fry the celeriac strips until crisp and golden brown for about 5 minutes. Drain and keep warm on a plate lined with kitchen paper.

3 Heat the remaining oil and stir-fry the onions, garlic and pepper for 2 minutes. Add the steak strips and fry for 3 minutes until browned.

4 Mix the beef stock, soy sauce and tomato puree together and add to the pan. Stir together then place on a serving platter and sprinkle the celeriac strips over the top. Serve with a rice or noodle dish.

# pork

# Five-spice Spare Ribs

*Easy Entertaining*

This favourite dish could not be easier to make, just marinade the spare ribs and bake them when you are ready.

### Ingredients for 2

**450g/1lb pork spare ribs**

**Marinade:**

- 1 tbsp rice wine or dry sherry
- 1 tbsp soy sauce
- 1 tbsp rice vinegar
- 2 tbsp hoisin sauce
- ½ tsp sesame oil
- 1 tsp five-spice powder
- 1 tbsp soft brown sugar
- 1 garlic clove, crushed
- 3 tbsp fresh orange juice

### Ingredients for 4

**900g/2lb pork spare ribs**

**Marinade:**

- 2 tbsp rice wine or dry sherry
- 2 tbsp soy sauce
- 2 tbsp rice vinegar
- 4 tbsp hoisin sauce
- 1 tsp sesame oil
- 2 tsp five-spice powder
- 2 tbsp soft brown sugar
- 2 garlic cloves, crushed
- 6 tbsp fresh orange juice

1 Separate the ribs by cutting down between the bones. Place the ribs in a large ovenproof baking dish.

2 Mix all the marinade ingredients together in a large jug and pour over the ribs in the dish. Cover with clingfilm and chill for 2-4 hours.

3 Preheat the oven to 180°C/350°F/Gas 4. Bake the ribs for 1 hour, then turn them over with a wooden spatula or fish slice.

4 Raise the heat to 220°C/425°F/Gas 7 and roast for a further 15-30 minutes until the ribs are tender and the marinade has baked into a sticky glaze. Serve with finger bowls and a slice of lemon.

# Sweet & Sour Pork

*Family Favourite*

## Ingredients for 2

175g/6oz pork fillet
1 tbsp rice wine or dry sherry
Oil for deep-frying

### Batter:

1/2 egg, beaten
1 tbsp cornflour, plus extra
for dusting

### Sauce:

1 tsp cornflour
5 tbsp chicken stock
1 tbsp tomato ketchup
1/2 tbsp sugar
1 tbsp soy sauce
1 tbsp rice vinegar
50g/2oz carrots, cut into
thin strips
25g/1oz spring onions,
thinly sliced
1/2 green pepper, cut into
small squares

## Ingredients for 4

350g/12oz pork fillet
2 tbsp rice wine or dry sherry
Oil for deep-frying

### Batter:

1 egg, beaten
2 tbsp cornflour, plus extra
for dusting

### Sauce:

2 tsp cornflour
150ml/1/4 pint chicken stock
2 tbsp tomato ketchup
1 tbsp sugar
2 tbsp soy sauce
1 1/2 tbsp rice vinegar
100g/4oz carrots, cut into
thin strips
50g/2oz spring onions,
thinly sliced
1 green pepper, cut into
small squares

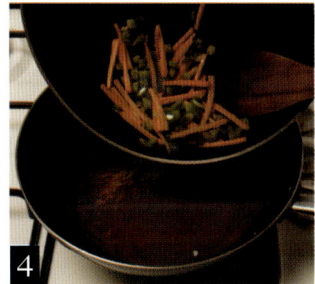

1 Cut the pork into 2.5cm/1 inch cubes, place in a bowl, sprinkle with rice wine or sherry and chill for 30 minutes.

2 In a bowl, whisk the egg and cornflour together into a light batter. Dust the pork cubes lightly in cornflour then dip into the batter.

3 Heat the oil for frying in a deep-fat fryer or wok. Fry the pork cubes until golden, then drain on kitchen paper and keep hot.

4 Make the sauce. Blend the cornflour with 2-3 tablespoons of cold water. Add the stock, ketchup, sugar, soy sauce and vinegar and heat until thickened. Stir-fry the carrots, onions, and pepper in a little oil for 3 minutes to soften. Add the sauce, stir to heat, then serve immediately with the pork and plain rice.

# Twice-cooked Pork

*Easy Entertaining*

This method of cooking, suited to cheaper cuts of meat, is popular in most Chinese households.

## Ingredients for 2

**500g/1lb 2oz belly of pork**
**500ml/18fl oz chicken stock**
**1 tbsp sunflower oil**
**2.5cm/1 inch root ginger,**
  **peeled and grated**
**1 clove garlic, chopped**
**2 tbsp sweet sherry**

## Ingredients for 4

**1kg/2¼ lb belly of pork**
**1ltr/1¾ pints chicken stock**
**1 tbsp sunflower oil**
**5cm/2 inch root ginger,**
  **peeled and grated**
**2 cloves garlic, chopped**
**4 tbsp sweet sherry**

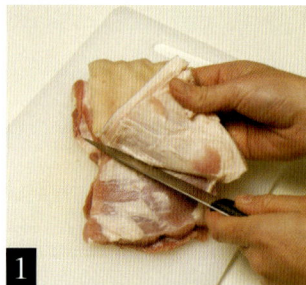

1 Preheat the oven to 190°C/375°F/Gas 5. Trim the pork of any excess fat and cut the meat into 4-8 large pieces.

2 Heat the stock to boiling in a large, ovenproof dish. Pour over the pork, cover with a lid or foil and bake for 45 minutes to 1 hour, or until tender.

3 Remove from the stock with a slotted spoon, drain and cut into 2.5cm/1 inch cubes, discarding any bones and fat.

4 Heat the oil in a wok or large frying pan and stir-fry the garlic and ginger for 1 minute. Add the pork and stir-fry for about 4 minutes until it turns golden. Add the sherry to the pan and cook for 2 minutes. Serve with an egg noodle dish.

# Pork Chop Suey

*Quick and Easy*

You can make this favourite stir-fry from any combination of vegetables you have available, by just slicing them all thinly and evenly.

## Ingredients for 2

100g/4oz pork fillet
1 tbsp soy sauce
1 tsp rice wine or sherry
1 tbsp cornflour
50g/2oz beansprouts
1/2 yellow or green pepper
2 spring onions
1cm/1/2 inch root ginger, peeled
1 carrot, peeled and thinly sliced
25g/1oz fine green beans, halved
4 tsp sunflower oil

## Ingredients for 4

225g/8oz pork fillet
2 tbsp soy sauce
1 tbsp rice wine or sherry
2 tbsp cornflour
100g/4oz beansprouts
1 yellow or green pepper
4 spring onions
2.5cm/1 inch root ginger, peeled
2 carrots, peeled and thinly sliced
50g/2oz fine green beans, halved
2 tbsp sunflower oil

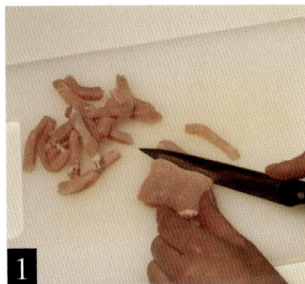

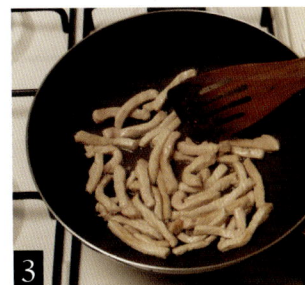

1 Cut the pork into thin slices and halve if the fillet is large. Mix the soy sauce, wine and cornflour together and coat the meat in the paste.

2 Wash the beansprouts in cold water and drain well. Remove the seeds from the pepper and cut into small diamonds. Slice the spring onions thinly and grate the ginger finely.

3 Heat half the oil in a wok or large frying pan. Stir-fry the pork slices for 3-4 minutes until golden, then remove from the pan with a slotted spoon.

4 Add the remaining oil and stir-fry the vegetables for 3-4 minutes. Return the pork slices to the pan and cook for a further minute, adding 1-2 tablespoons of water to moisten. Serve with plain boiled rice.

# Minced Pork Dumplings

*One Pot*

Dumplings may take a little time to prepare, but they are considered a real delicacy in China.

### Ingredients for 2

**225g/8oz pork mince**
**1 tbsp soy sauce**
**2 tsp rice wine or sherry**
**1 tsp sugar**
**½ egg**
**2 tsp cornflour**
**50g/2oz Chinese dried mushrooms**
**50g/2oz thin rice vermicelli noodles**
**1 tbsp sunflower oil**
**2.5cm/1 inch root ginger, peeled and sliced**
**1 spring onion, finely chopped**
**100g/4oz Chinese leaf, sliced**

### Ingredients for 4

**450g/1lb pork mince**
**2 tbsp soy sauce**
**1 tbsp rice wine or sherry**
**2 tsp sugar**
**1 egg**
**1 tbsp cornflour**
**100g/4oz Chinese dried mushrooms**
**100g/4oz thin rice vermicelli noodles**
**2 tbsp sunflower oil**
**5cm/2 inch root ginger, peeled and sliced**
**2 spring onions, finely chopped**
**225g/8oz Chinese leaf, sliced**

1 Mix the pork with the soy sauce, wine, sugar, egg and cornflour. Divide the mixture into 6 or 12 balls and refrigerate for 15 minutes.

2 Soak the dried mushrooms in warm water for 20 minutes, then drain and squeeze dry. Soak the rice noodles in water until soft.

3 Heat the oil in a large frying pan or wok and fry the meatballs until golden.

Remove from the pan with a slotted spoon.

4 Add the ginger and spring onions and stir-fry for 2 minutes. Add the Chinese leaf and mushrooms and stir-fry for 2 minutes. Return the meatballs to the pan with the noodles and 4-6 tablespoons of water. Simmer for 25 minutes until the meatballs are tender.

# Char Sui Roast Pork

*Easy Entertaining*

Marinating this dish gives the pork a delicious sweet-and-sour sticky coating.

## Ingredients for 2

2 pork shoulder steaks
Sichuan peppercorns,
   freshly ground
1 tbsp sunflower oil
1 tbsp dark soy sauce
1 tbsp Chinese red
   cooking wine
50g/2oz shallots, finely
   chopped
1 clove garlic, finely
   chopped
3 tbsp hoisin sauce
1 tbsp clear honey

## Ingredients for 4

4 pork shoulder steaks
Sichuan peppercorns,
   freshly ground
2 tbsp sunflower oil
2 tbsp dark soy sauce
2 tbsp Chinese red
   cooking wine
100g/4oz shallots, finely
   chopped
2 cloves garlic, finely
   chopped
6 tbsp hoisin sauce
2 tbsp clear honey

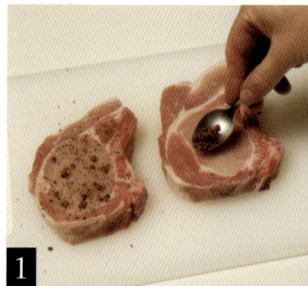

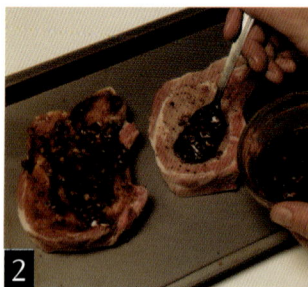

1 Season the steaks on both sides with the pepper and place them in a single layer in a roasting tin.

2 Mix the oil, soy sauce, wine, shallots, garlic and hoisin sauce together and spread over the steaks. Chill for 30 minutes.

3 Preheat the oven to 180°C/350°F/Gas 4. Drizzle the steaks with half the honey and roast for 20 minutes.

4 Turn the steaks over, spread with marinade from the tray and drizzle with remaining honey. Roast for a further 10-15 minutes until piping hot and browned. Serve with thin, boiled rice noodles and wilted pak choi.

# Pork & Mushroom Stir-fry

*Quick and Easy*

Thinly cut pork steaks cook so quickly, you can make this easy stir-fry in under 15 minutes.

## Ingredients for 2

225g/8oz thin cut, boneless
   pork loin steaks
2 tsp cornflour
1 tsp sesame oil
1 clove garlic, finely
   chopped
2.5cm/1 inch root ginger,
   peeled and grated
100g/4oz shitake mushrooms
4 tbsp rice wine or dry
   sherry
1 tbsp soy light sauce
50g/2oz small pak choi
   leaves
125g/4¹/₂oz egg noodles

## Ingredients for 4

450g/1lb thin cut, boneless
   pork loin steaks
4 tsp cornflour
2 tsp sesame oil
2 cloves garlic, finely
   chopped
5cm/2 inch root ginger,
   peeled and grated
225g/8oz shitake mushrooms
8 tbsp rice wine or dry
   sherry
2 tbsp soy light sauce
100g/4oz small pak choi
   leaves
250g/9oz egg noodles

1 Cut the pork into long, thin strips and toss them lightly in the cornflour to coat.

2 Heat the oil in a wok or large frying pan, add the garlic and ginger, and stir-fry for 1 minute. Add the pork strips and stir-fry for 3-4 minutes until browned and sealed.

3 Add the mushrooms and stir-fry for 1 minute. Add the wine, soy sauce and pak choi leaves and cook for a further 3-4 minutes.

4 Cook the egg noodles in boiling water according to the instructions on the pack, then drain and divide between four bowls. Top with the cooked pork, vegetables and juices from the pan and serve immediately.

# Roast Crispy Pork

*Easy Entertaining*

These delicious crispy strips of pork can be served hot or cold as a party platter for offering to guests with drinks.

## Ingredients for 2

**575g/1¼lb belly of pork, in one piece**
**2 tsp salt**
**1 tsp five-spice powder**

### To serve:

**4 tbsp soy sauce to serve**
**Chilli dipping sauce**

## Ingredients for 4

**1kg/2¼lb belly of pork, in one piece**
**3 tsp salt**
**2 tsp five-spice powder**

### To serve:

**8 tbsp soy sauce to serve**
**Chilli dipping sauce**

1 Dry the pork skin well, patting with kitchen paper. Mix the salt and the five-spice powder together and rub the mixture all over the meat. Leave to stand in a dish for 1 hour.

2 Preheat the oven to 220°C/425°F/Gas 7. Place the pork, skin side up, on a wire trivet in a large roasting dish.

3 Half-fill the roasting dish with boiling water. Roast the pork for 20 minutes then reduce the heat to 200°C/400°F/Gas 6.

4 Roast the meat for a further 40-45 minutes or until the skin has become crackling. Remove from the rack, place on a chopping board and carve into slices. Serve the slices on a platter, hot or cold, with dipping sauces. Accompany with pickled vegetables or a warm Chinese salad dish.

# Red Cooked Pork

*Family Favourite*

This pork braise is delicately simmered with five-spice powder. It is made from ground cinnamon, cloves, fennel seed, star anise and Sichuan peppercorns. It is particularly good with pork dishes, as it adds both a sweet and spicy flavour.

## Ingredients for 2

**450g/1lb lean pork**
**1 clove garlic, chopped**
**2 tbsp dark soy sauce**
**2 tbsp red rice wine or dry
    sherry**
**25g/1oz demerara sugar**
**1 tsp five-spice paste or
    powder**
**Spring onion tassels to
    garnish**

## Ingredients for 4

**900g/2lb lean pork**
**1 clove garlic, chopped**
**4 tbsp dark soy sauce**
**3 tbsp red rice wine or dry
    sherry**
**50g/2oz demerara sugar**
**2 tsp five-spice paste or
    powder**
**Spring onion tassels to
    garnish**

1 Cut the pork into 3cm/1¹/₂ inch cubes and place in a heavy-based saucepan.

2 Pour over enough cold water to cover the pork cubes.

3 Add the garlic, soy sauce, rice wine or sherry, sugar and five-spice and stir well. Bring to the boil then reduce the heat and cover the pan.

4 Simmer over a low heat for about 1 hour 15 minutes, until the pork is tender and there is only a little liquid left in the pan. Serve with a vegetable dish and egg noodles.

# Chilli Pork

*Hot and spicy*

This quick and easy dish makes a good midweek supper for the whole family.

## Ingredients for 2

**2 tsp sunflower oil**
**1 clove garlic, peeled and chopped**
**2.5cm/1 inch root ginger, peeled and grated**
**1 red chilli, seeded and chopped**
**175g/6oz lean minced pork**
**1 small red pepper, sliced**
**1 tbsp dark soy sauce**
**1 tbsp tomato puree**
**175g/6oz medium egg noodles**
**1 tsp sesame oil**
**1 tbsp fresh coriander leaves, chopped**

## Ingredients for 4

**1 tbsp sunflower oil**
**2 cloves garlic, peeled and chopped**
**5cm/2 inch root ginger, peeled and grated**
**2 red chillies, seeded and chopped**
**350g/12oz lean minced pork**
**1 red pepper, sliced**
**2 tbsp dark soy sauce**
**2 tbsp tomato puree**
**350g/12oz medium egg noodles**
**2 tsp sesame oil**
**2 tbsp fresh coriander leaves, chopped**

1 Heat the oil in a wok or a large frying pan and stir-fry the garlic, ginger and chilli for 2 minutes.

2 Add the pork and stir-fry until browned for 5 minutes. Add the red pepper and stir-fry for 2-3 minutes.

3 Add the soy sauce, puree and 4-6 tablespoons of water and cook over a low heat for 10 minutes. Cook the egg noodles in boiling water according to the instructions on the pack and drain in a sieve.

4 Add the sesame oil to the sieve and toss the noodles. Divide the noodles between warmed serving bowls and top with the cooked pork. Toss together, then serve sprinkled with chopped coriander.

# buffet
# specials

# Bang Bang Chicken

*Easy Entertaining*

This is a cold chicken dish from Sichuan. It makes a marvellous buffet or summer supper dish that can be prepared well ahead of time.

## Ingredients for 4

1.5kg/3lb 8oz whole chicken
1 long strip of lemon rind
2 bay leaves
1 crisp cos lettuce
1 large cucumber, peeled

## Sauce

5 tbsp peanut butter
2 tbsp sesame oil
1 tsp caster sugar
1/2 tsp salt
2 tsp tabasco sauce
1 tbsp sunflower oil
Red bird's-eye chillies to
     garnish

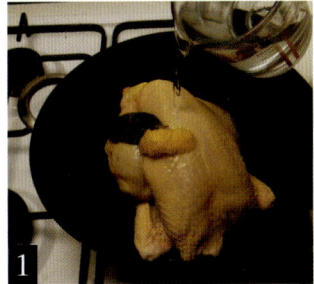

1 Wash the chicken and place in a large pan with the lemon rind and bay leaves, adding enough water to cover. Bring to the boil, then simmer with the lid on for 50 minutes, until poached and tender.

2 Remove the chicken from the stock, reserve the stock and cool. Skin the chicken, then take the meat off the bones and cut into 6mm/1/4 inch thick slices.

3 Wash and dry the lettuce then roll up the leaves and shred into ribbons. Place in one layer on a large serving platter. Shred the cucumber thinly by hand or in a food processor and arrange on top of the lettuce. Arrange the cold, sliced chicken on top of the cucumbers.

4 Place all the sauce ingredients into a saucepan with 175ml/6fl oz cooking stock or water and stir together. Bring to the boil, stirring until the sauce becomes smooth and shiny. Cool slightly, then drizzle over the chicken slices on the platter. Cut down each chilli to make flowers for garnishing and chill until needed for serving.

# Peking Duck

*Easy Entertaining*

This must be everybody's favourite – succulent pieces of duck with crispy skin and plum sauce, rolled up in wafer-thin pancakes.

### Ingredients for 4

**2.30 kg/5lb fresh, plump duck**
**1.2ltr/2 pint boiling water**

### Marinade

**90ml/3fl oz clear honey**
**2 tbsp dark soy sauce**
**90ml/3fl oz boiling water**

### To serve

**12-16 Pancakes (see page 68)**

### Plum sauce

**½ cucumber, cut into thin strips**
**100g/4oz spring onions, thinly sliced**

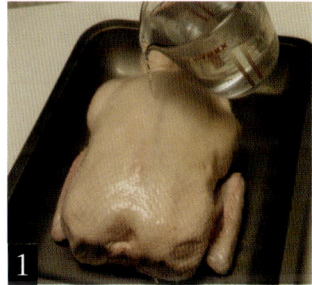

1 Place the duck on its back in a large casserole dish. Slowly pour the boiling water over the duck until the skin is almost white. Remove the duck, drain and pat dry with kitchen paper.

2 Hang the duck on a meat hook or attach it with string and leave overnight in a cool, airy place to dry out. Place a tray underneath for drips.

3 Mix all the marinade ingredients together and brush all over the duck's skin to cover completely. Leave to dry for 1 hour. Repeat until all the marinade has been used.

4 Preheat the oven to 190°C/375°F/Gas 5. Place the duck on a rack in a roasting tin and cook, uncovered for 1 hour 40 minutes until dark brown.

5 Peel the skin from the duck with a sharp knife. Carve the meat thinly and arrange, with the skin on a serving platter. To serve, spread each pancake with plum sauce, sprinkle over some duck meat and skin, cucumber strips and spring onions. Roll up each pancake and eat with your fingers.

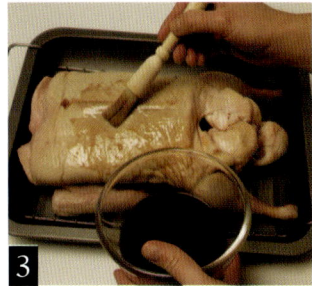

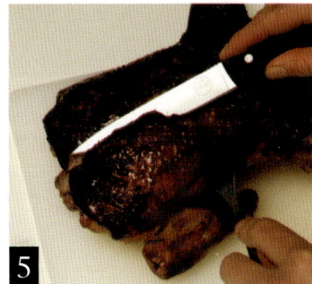

# Barbecued Pork Fillets

*Easy Entertaining*

If you take a trip through Chinatown, you will see these bright red, char sui marinated fillets hanging up in shop windows.

### Ingredients for 2

**375g/12oz pork fillet**

### Marinade:

**1 tbsp clear honey**
**1 tbsp sweet sherry**
**1/2 tbsp soft dark brown sugar**
**1/2 tbsp dark soy sauce**
**1 tbsp hoisin sauce**
**1 tsp red Chinese vinegar**
**1 tsp red bean paste**
**1/2 tsp five-spice paste or powder**
**1 clove garlic, chopped**

### Ingredients for 4

**2 pork fillets, each weighing 375g/12oz**

### Marinade:

**2 tbsp clear honey**
**2 tbsp sweet sherry**
**1 tbsp soft dark brown sugar**
**1 tbsp dark soy sauce**
**2 tbsp hoisin sauce**
**2 tsp red Chinese vinegar**
**2 tsp red bean paste**
**1 tsp five-spice paste or powder**
**2 cloves garlic, chopped**

1 Mix the marinade ingredients together in a large non-metallic bowl. Spread the marinade over the fillets to coat, cover with clingfilm and chill for 12-24 hours.

2 Preheat the oven to 190°C/375°F/Gas 5. Place the fillets on a wire rack in a roasting dish, reserving any marinade from the dish.

3 Bake the fillets for 15 minutes, turn them over and bake for a further 15 minutes. Brush with the reserved marinade then bake for a further 15 minutes.

4 Place the hot fillets on a chopping board and cut thinly across the grain into 1cm/1/2 inch thick slices. Serve hot on a platter with the slices overlapping.

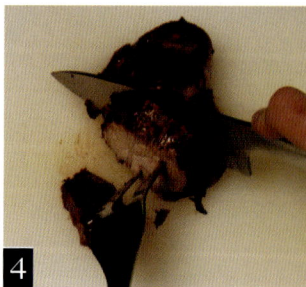

# Five Willow Fish

*Easy Entertaining*

China has a long coastline, so fish is plentiful and eaten in abundance. Steaming is a popular method of cooking in China as it retains the delicate flavours and texture of the fish.

## Ingredients for 2

**2 large dried Chinese mushrooms**
**One whole 450g/1lb sea bass, cleaned and scaled**
**5cm/2 inch root ginger, peeled and sliced**
**2 spring onions**
**50g/2oz cooked ham**
**50g/2oz bamboo shoots**
**3 tbsp rice wine or dry sherry**
**2 tbsp light soy sauce**
**1 tsp caster sugar**
**1/2 tsp salt**

## Ingredients for 4

**4 large dried Chinese mushrooms**
**Two whole 450g/1lb sea bass, cleaned and scaled**
**10cm/4 inch root ginger, peeled and sliced**
**4 spring onions**
**100g/4oz cooked ham**
**100g/4oz bamboo shoots**
**6 tbsp rice wine or dry sherry**
**4 tbsp light soy sauce**
**2 tsp caster sugar**
**1 tsp salt**

1 Soak the mushrooms in warm water for 20 minutes and squeeze them dry. If the fish is large, remove the head. Cut slashes into both sides of the fish diagonally about 1cm/1/2 inch deep. Place the fish on a large piece of foil or a plate that will fit inside a steamer.

2 Cut the mushrooms, ginger, spring onions, ham and bamboo shoots into thin shreds. Place the mixture on top of the fish.

3 Mix together the wine or sherry, soy sauce, sugar and salt in a small jug and pour over the fish.

4 Place boiling water in a large saucepan or wok and place the steamer on top, cover with a lid or foil and steam for 15 minutes, or until tender. Serve the fish with the liquor from the plate and its topping.

# Tiger Whisker Salad

### Easy Entertaining

The thinly shredded vegetables in this salad represent the whiskers of a tiger.

## Ingredients for 2

**225g/8oz lean rump steak,
   top rump or topside**
**2 tbsp sunflower oil**
**2.5cm/1 inch root ginger,
   peeled**
**1 clove garlic, peeled and
   chopped**
**3 spring onions, shredded**
**25g/1oz carrots, cut into
   thin shreds**
**25g/1oz beansprouts**
**25g/1oz mangetout, halved
   if large**
**1 tbsp soy sauce**

## Ingredients for 4

**450g/1lb lean rump steak, top
   rump or topside**
**4 tbsp sunflower oil**
**5cm/2 inch root ginger,
   peeled**
**2 cloves garlic, peeled and
   chopped**
**6 spring onions, shredded**
**50g/2oz carrots, cut into
   thin shreds**
**50g/2oz beansprouts**
**50g/2oz mangetout, halved
   if large**
**1 tbsp soy sauce**

1 Wrap the steak in clingfilm and half freeze for 20 minutes to firm the meat. Cut the meat into strips about 2.5cm/1 inch wide, then cut across the grain into strips 3mm/1/8 inch wide. Cut the strips into matchstick shreds 3mm/1/8 inch thick.

2 Heat the oil in a wok or large frying pan and stir-fry the meat in batches for about 1 minute each batch. Remove with a slotted spoon and drain.

3 Add the remaining oil and add the garlic, ginger and spring onions for 1 minute. Add the carrot, beansprouts and mangetout and stir-fry for 1 minute only, keeping the vegetables crisp.

4 Add the soy sauce and 1 tablespoon of water, return the meat to the pan and stir-fry for 1 minute only. Serve the salad warm or cold on a serving platter.

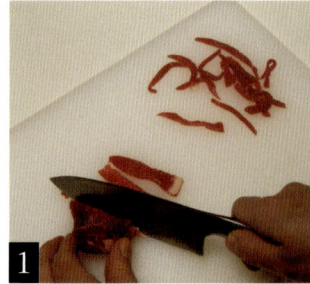

# Dragon Tooth Salad

*vegetarian*

This crunchy salad makes a colourful addition to any buffet.

## Ingredients for 2

1 small mooli
2 spring onions
8 baby sweetcorn cobs
2 tsp sunflower oil
1 clove garlic, peeled and
   finely chopped
2.5cm/1 inch root ginger,
   sliced
1 tbsp yellow bean sauce
1 red pepper, thinly sliced
50g/2oz beansprouts
25g/1oz mangetout
1 tsp sesame oil
Fresh coriander to garnish

## Ingredients for 4

1 large mooli
4 spring onions
16 baby sweetcorn cobs
1 tbsp sunflower oil
2 cloves garlic, peeled and
   finely chopped
3 cm/1½ inch root ginger,
   sliced
2 tbsp yellow bean sauce
1 red pepper, thinly sliced
100g/4oz beansprouts
50g/2oz mangetout
2 tsp sesame oil
Fresh coriander to garnish

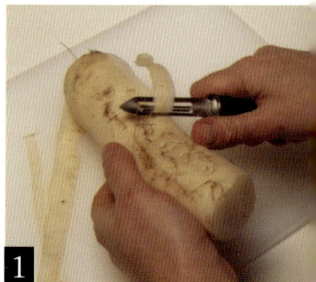

1 Scrape the mooli and cut into strips 1cm/¹/₂ inch wide by 5cm/2 inch long. Cut the spring onions into 5cm/2 inch long strips.

2 Bring a pan of salted water to the boil. Add the sweetcorn cobs and blanch for 2 minutes. Drain and plunge into cold water. Drain well.

3 Heat the oil in a wok or large frying pan, add the

garlic and ginger and stir-fry for 1 minute to soften. Add the yellow bean sauce and 6 tablespoons of cold water and bring to the boil.

4 Add all the vegetables to the pan and stir in the hot liquid for 1 minute until the vegetables are just softening. Turn off the heat, stir in the sesame oil and spoon onto a serving platter. Serve sprinkled with fresh coriander.

# Sweet & Sour Beancurd Salad

*vegetarian*

This tangy main course, based around tofu, is ideal to serve to vegetarian guests.

## Ingredients for 2

**225g/8oz beancurd or tofu**
**50g/2oz thin egg noodles**
**1 tbsp vegetable oil**
**1 clove garlic, peeled and chopped**
**1 carrot, cut into thin matchsticks**
**1 small green pepper, thinly sliced**
**50g/2oz beansprouts**
**50g/2oz bamboo shoots**

### Sauce:

**2 tsp cornflour**
**1 tbsp soft light brown sugar**
**1 tbsp rice vinegar**
**125ml/4fl oz vegetable stock**
**2 tsp tomato puree**

## Ingredients for 4

**450g/1lb beancurd or tofu**
**100g/4oz thin egg noodles**
**2 tbsp vegetable oil**
**2 cloves garlic, peeled and chopped**
**2 carrots, cut into thin matchsticks**
**1 large green pepper, thinly sliced**
**100g/4oz beansprouts**
**100g/4oz bamboo shoots**

### Sauce:

**1 tbsp cornflour**
**2 tbsp soft light brown sugar**
**2 tbsp rice vinegar**
**225ml/8floz vegetable stock**
**1 tbsp tomato puree**

1 Cut the beancurd into large 5cm/2 inch cubes. Break the dry noodles into short strands and cook in boiling salted water for 3 minutes until soft, then drain.

2 Heat the oil in a large pan or wok and fry the garlic for 1 minute to soften. Add the carrots, pepper, beansprouts and bamboo shoots and stir-fry for 4 minutes. Add the beancurd and cook for a further 2 minutes.

3 Mix the cornflour to a paste with 2 tablespoons of water then combine in a jug with all the remaining ingredients.

4 Add the cooked noodles to the pan and pour in the sauce. Stir well and cook over a high heat until the liquid boils and thickens for 1 minute, then serve immediately.

# Honeyed Chicken Wings

*Hot and spicy*

Chicken wings are an ideal choice for a buffet party, and they are so economical they won't break the bank.

## Ingredients for 2

1 small chilli, seeded and
   finely chopped
1/2 tsp chilli powder
1/2 tsp ground ginger
Finely grated zest of 1/2 lemon
6 chicken wing joints
2 tbsp sunflower oil
1 tbsp soy sauce
3 tbsp clear honey
1 tbsp fresh coriander
Lemon twists to decorate

## Ingredients for 4

1 red chilli, seeded and finely
   chopped
1 tsp chilli powder
1 tsp ground ginger
Finely grated zest of 1 lemon
12 chicken wing joints
4 tbsp sunflower oil
2 tbsp soy sauce
6 tbsp clear honey
1 tbsp fresh coriander
Lemon twists to decorate

1 Mix the chopped chilli, chilli powder, ground ginger and lemon zest together and rub into the chicken joints. Chill for 1 hour.

2 Heat half the oil in a wok or large pan and fry the chicken wings in batches of 3 or 4 on both sides for 10 minutes, turning regularly. Continue cooking all the wings, adding the remaining oil with each batch.

3 Return all the wings to the wok and add the soy sauce and honey. Stir-fry for 2 minutes until the wings are coated.

4 Add the chopped coriander to the pan and stir-fry for 1 minute, turning regularly. Place the wings on a serving platter and serve hot or cold, garnished with lemon twists.

# Sichuan Chilli Prawns

Hot and spicy

These fiery prawns are not for the faint-hearted! Serve them with drinks, or as part of a cold buffet.

## Ingredients for 2

**225g/8oz large raw tiger prawns with tails attached**
**1 tbsp sunflower oil**
**2 cloves of garlic, peeled and finely chopped**
**1 small onion, peeled and finely chopped**
**1 red chilli, seeded and chopped**
**1/2 tsp chilli powder**
**1/2 tsp five-spice powder**
**Fresh coriander and lemon twists to serve**

## Ingredients for 4

**450g/1lb large raw tiger prawns with tails attached**
**2 tbsp sunflower oil**
**4 cloves of garlic, peeled and finely chopped**
**1 onion, peeled and finely chopped**
**2 red chillies, seeded and chopped**
**1 tsp chilli powder**
**1 tsp five-spice powder**
**Fresh coriander and lemon twists to serve**

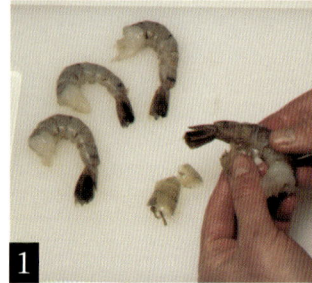

1 If necessary remove the heads, any shells and the black veins from the backs of the prawns. Wash the prawns and pat completely dry on kitchen paper.

2 Heat the oil in a wok or large frying pan and fry the garlic and onion for 3 minutes to soften.

3 Add the chillies, chilli powder and five-spice powder. Stir-fry for 30 seconds then add 6 tablespoons of water to make a thick sauce.

4 Add the prawns and stir-fry for 3-4 minutes until the prawns turn pink and the sauce is hot and bubbling, adding extra water if necessary. Place a toothpick in each prawn and serve on a platter, sprinkled with fresh coriander.

# Hot & Sour Beef

*Easy Entertaining*

Serve these tender slices with drinks, or as a delicious light main course.

## Ingredients for 2

**175g/6oz fillet or sirloin
    steak
1 tsp cumin seeds
1/2 tsp ground cinnamon
Sea salt and freshly ground
    Sichuan pepper
1 tbsp sunflower oil**

### Dressing:

**1 lime
1 tbsp soy sauce
1 tbsp fresh coriander,
    chopped
1 tsp fish sauce
1 small red chilli, seeded
    and finely chopped**

## Ingredients for 4

**350g/12oz fillet or sirloin
    steak
2 tsp cumin seeds
1 tsp ground cinnamon
Sea salt and freshly ground
    Sichuan pepper
2 tbsp sunflower oil**

### Dressing:

**2 limes
2 tbsp soy sauce
2 tbsp fresh coriander,
    chopped
2 tsp fish sauce
1 large red chilli, seeded
    and finely chopped**

1 Pound the cumin seed to a powder with the cinnamon in a pestle and mortar, or in a small food mill or processor.

2 Season the steak with salt and pepper and coat the outside in the dry spice mix. Heat the oil in a wok or large frying pan and sear the steaks for 2 minutes on each side.

3 Remove from the wok, cool and chill the meat for at least 1 hour in the refrigerator. To make the dressing, squeeze the juice from the limes and mix with the remaining ingredients and chill.

4 With a very sharp knife, cut the steak into wafer thin strips. Thread the strips onto wooden skewers and place on a serving platter with mixed salad leaves. Sprinkle half the dressing over the meat and serve the remainder in a dipping bowl.

# noodles *and* rice

# Singapore Noodles

*Hot and Spicy*

This dish combines the flavours and spices of two continents, India and China.

## Ingredients for 2

100g/4oz thin rice noodles
2 eggs, beaten
1 tsp sesame oil
1 tbsp sunflower oil
1 clove garlic, peeled and
    chopped
1 small green chilli, seeded
    and sliced
2 spring onions
50g/2oz Chinese barbecue
    pork, finely chopped
50g/2oz prawns, peeled
2 canned water chestnuts,
    drained and chopped
50g/2oz frozen peas

### Sauce:

1 tbsp soy sauce
1 tbsp medium Indian curry
    paste
1 tbsp rice wine or dry sherry
125ml/4fl oz coconut milk

## Ingredients for 4

225g/8oz thin rice noodles
4 eggs, beaten
2 tsp sesame oil
2 tbsp sunflower oil
2 cloves garlic, peeled and
    chopped
2 small green chillies,
    seeded and sliced
4 spring onions
100g/4oz Chinese barbecue
    pork, finely chopped
100g/4oz prawns, peeled
4 canned water chestnuts,
    drained and chopped
100g/4oz frozen peas

### Sauce:

2 tbsp soy sauce
2 tbsp medium Indian curry
    paste
2 tbsp rice wine or dry sherry
250ml/9fl oz coconut milk

1 Soak the noodles in hot water for 20 minutes then drain. Beat the eggs with the sesame oil and season with salt and pepper.

2 Heat the sunflower oil in a wok or large frying pan. Add the garlic, chilli and spring onions and stir-fry for 2 minutes.

3 Add the pork, prawns and peas and stir-fry for 1 minute. Whisk all the sauce ingredients together in a jug, then pour into the pan.

4 Cook over a high heat for 5 minutes, stirring until most of the liquid evaporates. Add the egg mixture and stir fry for 1-2 minutes until the egg has set. Add the drained noodles. Serve immediately.

# Chow Mein

*One Pot*

This is one of the most popular Chinese dishes, and very versatile. Make it with chicken, pork or beef.

## Ingredients for 2

100g/4oz medium egg
   noodles
4 tsp sesame oil
50g/2oz chicken breast,
   skinned and boned
1 tbsp sunflower oil
1 clove garlic, peeled and
   chopped
2 spring onions, thinly sliced
1 celery stick, thinly sliced
25g/1oz mangetout
2 tsp rice wine or dry
   sherry
1 tbsp soy sauce

## Ingredients for 4

225g/8oz medium egg
   noodles
2 tsp sesame oil
100g/4oz chicken breast,
   skinned and boned
2 tbsp sunflower oil
2 cloves garlic, peeled and
   chopped
4 spring onions, thinly sliced
2 celery sticks, thinly sliced
50g/2oz mangetout
1 tbsp rice wine or dry
   sherry
2 tbsp soy sauce

1 Cook the egg noodles in boiling, salted water, according to the instructions on the pack . Drain, then plunge into cold water and drain again. Toss in half the sesame oil in a colander.

2 Cut the chicken into long, thin shreds. Heat the oil in a wok or deep frying pan and stir-fry the chicken for 1-2 minutes, remove from the pan and keep warm. Add the garlic, spring onions, and celery to the wok and stir-fry for 2 minutes to soften.

3 Add the mangetout and stir-fry for 1 minute, then add the rice wine and soy sauce.

4 Add the cooked noodles and chicken with the remaining sesame oil and toss together. Serve immediately.

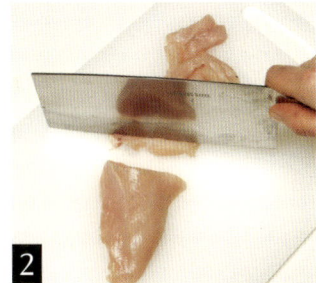

# Hot Noodles with Chilli Beef

Hot and spicy

This warming dish is a meal in itself, served all in one bowl.

## Ingredients for 2

50g/2oz ribbon cellophane
    or bean thread noodles
2 tsp sunflower oil
2 spring onions
1 clove garlic, chopped
175g/6oz extra lean
    minced beef
1/2 tsp chilli powder
1 tbsp yellow bean sauce
1 tbsp soy sauce
225ml/8fl oz chicken stock
1 tsp sesame oil
1 tbsp freshly chopped
    coriander

## Ingredients for 4

100g/4oz ribbon cellophane
    or bean thread noodles
1 tbsp sunflower oil
4 spring onions
2 cloves garlic, chopped
350g/12oz extra lean
    minced beef
1 tsp chilli powder
2 tbsp yellow bean sauce
2 tbsp soy sauce
450ml/3/4 pint chicken stock
2 tsp sesame oil
2 tbsp freshly chopped
    coriander

1 Place the noodles in a bowl and pour hot water over to cover. Soak the noodles for 15 minutes until they are soft. Drain and cut into 7.5cm/3 inch lengths with kitchen scissors.

2 Heat the oil in a wok or large frying pan, add the onions and garlic and stir-fry for 2 minutes to soften. Add the minced beef and the chilli powder and stir-fry to brown for 5 minutes.

3 Add the sauces and the stock and simmer for 10-15 minutes until the meat is tender and half the liquid has evaporated.

4 Toss the cooked noodles in the sesame oil and add to the pan. Stir fry for 3-4 minutes until thoroughly heated, then serve hot in individual bowls topped with fresh coriander.

# Crispy Noodles

*Family Favourite*

Use these fluffy noodles for serving on top of beef or chicken dishes with plenty of sauce.

## Ingredients for 2

**150g/5oz medium egg noodles**
**Oil for deep-fat frying**

## Ingredients for 4

**275g/10oz medium egg noodles**
**Oil for deep-fat frying**

1 Bring a large pan of water to the boil and plunge in the noodles. Break the noodles up to separate. Boil for 2 minutes then rinse under cold running water and drain thoroughly.

2 Heat the oil in a deep-fat fryer to 190°C/375°F, or set to the potato chip frying setting if you have an electric deep-fat fryer. Separate the noodles into bundles.

3 Lower one bundle of noodles into the hot oil in a frying basket, or with a large slotted frying spoon. The noodles will puff out and expand very quickly.

4 Remove from the oil with a slotted spoon after 30 seconds and shake to remove excess oil. Drain on kitchen paper and keep warm in a serving bowl in the oven. In the meantime, fry the remaining noodles in batches.

# Simple Plain Rice

*Quick and Easy*

Plain rice is ideal to serve with hot and spicy dishes, but also forms the basis for fried and flavoured rice dishes.

## Ingredients for 2

**150g/6oz American long grain rice**
**1/2 tsp salt**
**1 tsp sunflower oil**

## Ingredients for 4

**350/12oz American long grain rice**
**1 tsp salt**
**2 tsp sunflower oil**

1 Measure the rice into a jug, make a note of the level then pour it into a saucepan with the salt and oil.

2 Fill the jug with cold water up to the level of the rice. Pour the water into the pan with the rice, then fill the jug to the same level again so that you have twice the volume of water to rice. Add the water to the pan and bring to the boil.

3 Turn the heat down to a low setting and simmer gently for 12-14 minutes when the liquid should be absorbed and the rice will look dry.

4 Switch off the heat and leave the rice to stand for 5 minutes covered with kitchen paper to absorb any steam. Transfer to a warmed bowl to serve and break up any large lumps with a fork to fluff the rice. Serve immediately.

### Cook's tip:

Don't use quick-cook, easy-cook or precooked long grain rice for these recipes. These grains are meant for quick cooking and may go mushy, meaning that the rice will not separate. If you can't find ordinary American long grain rice, use basmati rice instead.

# Curried Rice

Hot and spicy

This hot and spicy dish goes well with pork dishes such as spare ribs.

### Ingredients for 2

**1 tbsp sunflower oil**
**1 small clove garlic, chopped**
**1 small red chilli, chopped**
**1 tbsp medium Indian**
**curry paste**
**175g/6oz plain rice, cooked**
**(see page 198)**
**1 tbsp soy sauce**
**50g/2oz frozen green**
**beans, chopped**
**Pinch of salt**
**1/2 tsp caster sugar**
**Pine nuts to decorate**

### Ingredients for 4

**2 tbsp sunflower oil**
**1 clove garlic, chopped**
**1 red chilli, chopped**
**2 tbsp medium Indian**
**curry paste**
**350/12oz plain rice, cooked**
**(see page 198)**
**2 tbsp soy sauce**
**100g/4oz frozen green**
**beans, chopped**
**Pinch of salt**
**1 tsp caster sugar**
**Pine nuts to decorate**

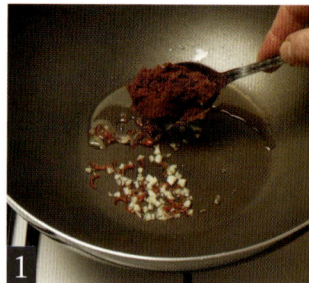

1 Heat the oil in a wok or large frying pan. Add the garlic and chilli and stir-fry for 1 minute. Add the curry paste and stir for a further minute to cook the raw spices in the paste.

2 Add the rice and stir-fry in the curry paste for 1 minute, stirring frequently to coat all the grains.

3 Add the soy sauce and the frozen beans and cook for 3 minutes, stirring regularly.

4 Season with salt and sugar and place in warmed serving bowls. Decorate with pine nuts.

# Egg Fried Rice

*Family Favourite*

Dishes with strips of omelette are popular in Chinese cooking and make plain rice dishes extra special.

## Ingredients for 2

1 tbsp sunflower oil
1/2 tsp sesame oil
1 large egg, beaten
2 spring onions, sliced
50g/2oz beansprouts
50g/2oz frozen peas
175g/6oz cooked plain rice
(see page 198)
1 tbsp light soy sauce
25g/1oz Char sui pork or
cooked ham, diced

## Ingredients for 4

2 tbsp sunflower oil
1 tsp sesame oil
2 eggs, beaten
4 spring onions, sliced
100g/4oz beansprouts
75g/3oz frozen peas
350g/12oz cooked plain rice
(see page 198)
2 tbsp light soy sauce
50g/2oz Char sui pork or
cooked ham, diced

1 Heat half the sunflower oil in a large frying pan or wok and pour in the beaten egg. Tilt the pan so that the egg covers the base to make a thin pancake. Cook for 1 minute then turn the pancake over and cook for a further minute until golden. Turn out onto a plate to cool.

2 Heat the remaining oils in the pan and add the onions, beansprouts and peas. Stir-fry for 3 minutes to soften.

3 Add the cooked rice to the pan and stir-fry for 3 minutes, stirring frequently.

4 Add the soy sauce and the pork or ham and stir-fry for 1 minute. Cut the omelette into thin strips. Scatter the strips into the hot rice. Serve in warmed bowls, immediately.

# Vegetable Fried Rice

*vegetarian*

Serve this rice with vegetarian dishes. You can vary the vegetables, as long as they are all cut to a similar size so that they will take the same amount of time to cook.

## Ingredients for 2

2 tbsp sunflower oil
1 clove garlic, peeled and chopped
1cm/1/2 inch root ginger, peeled and chopped
2 spring onions, sliced
1/2 red or orange pepper, seeded and sliced
1 carrot, peeled and sliced into matchsticks
50g/2oz baby corncobs
25g/1oz canned bamboo shoots, drained
25g/1oz frozen green beans, halved
175g/6oz cooked plain rice, (see page 198)
1 tsp sesame oil

## Ingredients for 4

3 tbsp sunflower oil
2 cloves garlic, peeled and chopped
2.5cm/1 inch root ginger, peeled and chopped
4 spring onions, sliced
1 red or orange pepper, seeded and sliced
1 carrot, peeled and sliced into matchsticks
100g/4oz baby corncobs
50g/2oz canned bamboo shoots, drained
50g/2oz frozen green beans, halved
350g/12oz cooked plain rice, (see page 198)
1 tsp sesame oil

1 Heat the oil in a large wok or frying pan and fry the garlic, ginger and spring onions for 1 minute.

2 Add the pepper, and carrot and cook for a further 2 minutes to soften.

3 Add the corncobs, bamboo shoots and green beans and stir-fry for 2 minutes.

4 Add the rice and sesame oil and stir-fry for 3 minutes until the rice is thoroughly heated, stirring constantly.

# Jewelled Rice

*Easy Entertaining*

This dish is so-called because of the many colours in the rice.

## Ingredients for 2

2 dried black mushrooms
2 tbsp vegetable oil
175g/6oz cooked plain rice,
    (see page 198)
1 small red onion, sliced
50g/2oz frozen peas
50g/2oz cooked ham, diced
75g/3oz canned white crab
    meat
50g/2oz canned water
    chestnuts, drained and
    diced
1 tbsp oyster sauce
Chillies to garnish

## Ingredients for 4

4 dried black mushrooms
3 tbsp vegetable oil
350g/12oz cooked plain rice,
    (see page 198)
1 medium red onion, sliced
100g/4oz frozen peas
100g/4oz cooked ham, diced
175g/6oz canned white crab
    meat
100g/4oz canned water
    chestnuts, drained and
    diced
2 tbsp oyster sauce
Chilles to garnish

1 Place the dried mushrooms in warm water and leave to soak for 20 minutes. Drain, then slice thinly.

2 Heat half the oil in a wok or large frying pan and stir-fry the cooked rice for 2-3 minutes. Empty into a bowl and keep warm.

3 Add the remaining oil to the pan and stir-fry the onion and mushrooms for 2 minutes to soften. Add the peas and cook for 1 minute.

4 Return the rice to the pan and stir together with the ham, crab meat, water chestnuts and oyster sauce. Stir-fry for 2 minutes until thoroughly heated through, then serve in small bowls, garnished with chilli flowers.

# Cellophane Noodles

*Low Fat*

Cellophane noodles are made from rice flour and have a very delicate flavour that makes an ideal partner for seafood.

## Ingredients for 2

**75g/3oz flat cellophane noodles**
**1 tbsp sunflower oil**
**1 clove garlic, crushed**
**2.5cm/1 inch root ginger, peeled and chopped**
**1 small green pepper, seeded and chopped**
**1 small leek, washed and thinly sliced**
**12 raw tiger prawns, peeled and deveined**
**1 tsp chilli sauce**
**1 tbsp light soy sauce**
**1 tsp rice vinegar**
**Lemon twists to garnish**

## Ingredients for 4

**175g/6oz flat cellophane noodles**
**1 tbsp sunflower oil**
**1 clove garlic, crushed**
**5cm/2 inch root ginger, peeled and chopped**
**1 green pepper, seeded and chopped**
**1 leek, washed and thinly sliced**
**24 raw tiger prawns, peeled and deveined**
**2 tbsp chilli sauce**
**2 tbsp light soy sauce**
**2 tsp rice vinegar**
**Lemon twists to garnish**

1 Place the noodles in a large saucepan of boiling water and cook for 2 minutes. Drain, plunge into a bowl of cold water and rinse again.

2 Heat the oil in a wok and stir-fry the garlic, ginger, pepper and leek for 2 minutes.

3 Add the prawns and stir-fry for 1 minute until they turn pink.

4 Add the drained noodles with the sauces and vinegar. Cook for 1-2 minutes until heated through, then serve in warmed serving bowls topped with lemon twists.

# vegetables

# Soy Braised Chinese Leaf

*Quick and Easy*

Serve this simple vegetable with plain rice to accompany very spicy or fiery dishes.

## Ingredients for 2

**225g/8oz Chinese leaf**
**2 tsp sunflower oil**
**2 spring onions, sliced**
**1 clove garlic, peeled and**
**chopped**
**2 tbsp light soy sauce**
**2 tsp rice wine or dry sherry**
**2 tsp clear honey**
**1 tsp sesame oil**
**1 tbsp toasted sesame seeds**

## Ingredients for 4

**450g/1lb Chinese leaf**
**1 tbsp sunflower oil**
**4 spring onions, sliced**
**2 cloves garlic, peeled and**
**chopped**
**4 tbsp light soy sauce**
**1 tbsp rice wine or dry sherry**
**1 tbsp clear honey**
**1 tbsp sesame oil**
**2 tbsp toasted sesame seeds**

1. Separate the leaves and stack them one on top of the other. With a sharp knife, cut across the leaves to make thick shreds.

2. Heat the oil in a wok or large frying pan and add the onions and garlic. Stir-fry for 2 minutes to soften. Add the sliced leaves and stir-fry for 1 minute.

3. Add the soy sauce, wine and honey and cook for 2-3 minutes until the leaves begin to wilt.

4. Add the sesame oil and stir-fry for a minute, then spoon onto a warmed platter and serve sprinkled with sesame seeds.

# Steamed Cabbage Leaf Rolls

*vegetarian*

Serve these dainty little parcels as part of a vegetarian meal.

## Ingredients for 2

**4 large Chinese leaves**

### Filling:

- **1 clove garlic, peeled and chopped**
- **1cm/½ inch root ginger, peeled and grated**
- **1 small carrot**
- **1 stick celery**
- **2 spring onions**
- **1 tbsp salted peanuts**
- **2 water chestnuts, drained**
- **1 tbsp peanut butter**
- **1 tsp tomato puree**
- **1 tsp soy sauce**
- **½ tsp sesame oil**

## Ingredients for 4

**8 large Chinese leaves**

### Filling:

- **1 clove garlic, peeled and chopped**
- **2.5cm/1 inch root ginger, peeled and grated**
- **1 large carrot**
- **1 stick celery**
- **4 spring onions**
- **2 tbsp salted peanuts**
- **4 water chestnuts, drained**
- **2 tbsp peanut butter**
- **2 tsp tomato puree**
- **2 tsp soy sauce**
- **1 tsp sesame oil**

1 Bring a large pan of water to the boil and turn off the heat. Add the cabbage leaves and leave for 2 minutes to soften them, then drain in a colander.

2 Place the carrot, celery, onions, peanuts and water chestnuts in a food processor and chop finely (or chop finely by hand). Place in a bowl and mix with all the remaining ingredients.

3 Spread out the cabbage leaves and divide the filling between them. Fold the sides in and roll the leaves up to make neat parcels. Tie each parcel with fine string.

4 Place the parcels in a steamer set over a pan of boiling water and steam for 20 minutes. Serve with chilli dipping sauce or soy sauce.

# Beancurd Stir-fry

vegetarian

Coconut milk makes this dish smooth and creamy.

## Ingredients for 2

**100g/4oz firm beancurd**
**4 tsp sunflower oil**
**1 red chilli, seeded and chopped**
**1 clove garlic, peeled and chopped**
**2 spring onions, chopped**
**50g/2oz carrots, peeled and finely shredded**
**50g/2oz frozen fine green beans**
**50g/ 2oz baby sweetcorn cobs**
**50g/2oz beansprouts**
**1 tbsp soy sauce**
**2 tbsp peanut butter**
**150ml/¼ pint coconut milk**

## Ingredients for 4

**225g/8oz firm beancurd**
**3 tbsp sunflower oil**
**2 red chillies, seeded and chopped**
**2 cloves garlic, peeled and chopped**
**4 spring onions, chopped**
**100g/4oz carrots, peeled and finely shredded**
**100g/4oz frozen fine green beans**
**100g/4oz baby sweetcorn cobs**
**100g/4oz beansprouts**
**2 tbsp soy sauce**
**4 tbsp peanut butter**
**300ml/½ pint coconut milk**

1 Cut the beancurd into large cubes with a sharp knife. Heat half the oil in a wok or a large frying pan and fry for 3-4 minutes until browned all over. Remove to a plate to keep warm.

2 Add the remaining oil to the pan and stir-fry the chillies, garlic and onions for 1 minute. Add the carrots, beans, sweetcorn and beansprouts and stir-fry for 4 minutes until softened.

3 Whisk the soy sauce, peanut butter and coconut milk together in a jug and pour into the pan. Stir well and cook the vegetables for 3 minutes.

4 Add the cooked beancurd to the pan and cook for 1 minute until heated through. Serve immediately with a rice or noodle dish.

# Four Mushroom Dish

*Easy Entertaining*

The delicate textures and flavours of four types of mushrooms are combined in this rich and delicious accompaniment.

## Ingredients for 2

25g/1oz dried black
   mushrooms
1 tbsp sunflower oil
1 clove garlic, peeled and
   crushed
50g/2oz oyster mushrooms
50g/2oz brown cap
   mushrooms, sliced
50g/2oz large open flat
   mushrooms, sliced
1 tbsp dark soy sauce
1 tbsp rice wine or dry
   sherry
2 tbsp oyster sauce
1/2 tsp ground Sichuan pepper
1/2 tsp caster sugar
Chives to garnish

## Ingredients for 4

50g/2oz dried black
   mushrooms
2 tbsp sunflower oil
2 cloves garlic, peeled and
   crushed
100g/4oz oyster mushrooms
100g/4oz brown cap
   mushrooms, sliced
100g/4oz large open flat
   mushrooms, sliced
2 tbsp dark soy sauce
2 tbsp rice wine or dry
   sherry
4 tbsp oyster sauce
1 tsp ground Sichuan pepper
1 tsp caster sugar
Chives to garnish

1 Soak the dried mushrooms in warm water for 20 minutes. Drain the mushrooms and cut into fine shreds.

2 Heat the oil in a wok or a large frying pan and stir-fry the garlic for 1 minute. Add the mushrooms and stir-fry for 1-2 minutes to just soften.

3 Add the soy sauce, wine and oyster sauce and stir-fry to coat the mushrooms for 1 minute.

4 Season the mushrooms with the pepper and sugar, transfer to a serving dish and serve topped with snipped chives.

# Pak Choi Oyster Sauce

*Quick and Easy*

Oyster sauce gives a rich, savoury flavour to this delicate vegetable dish.

## Ingredients for 2

100g/4oz pak choi
2 tsp sunflower oil
1 clove garlic, peeled and
    sliced
1 small onion, peeled and
    thinly sliced
90ml/3fl oz vegetable stock
2 tbsp oyster sauce

## Ingredients for 4

225g/8oz pak choi
1 tbsp sunflower oil
2 cloves garlic, peeled and
    sliced
1 large onion, peeled and
    thinly sliced
175ml/6fl oz vegetable stock
4 tbsp oyster sauce

1 Separate the pak choi into leaves. Strip the green part away from the white stems with a sharp knife. Slice the white parts thinly.

2 Heat the oil and fry the white stems, garlic and sliced onions for 1-2 minutes to soften.

3 Add the stock and the oyster sauce to the pan, then add the pak choi leaves.

4 Stir well and cook over a low heat for 2-3 minutes until the leaves have just wilted. Serve immediately.

# Fried Noodles with Vegetables

*Easy Entertaining*

For a special treat for vegetarian guests, serve these crispy noodle nests, topped with tasty stir fried vegetables and a tangy sweet and sour sauce

## Ingredients for 2

**175g/6oz egg noodles**
**Oil for deep fat frying**
**1 tbsp sunflower oil**
**1 clove garlic, peeled and**
   **chopped**
**1 carrot, sliced into**
   **matchsticks**
**½ green pepper, thinly sliced**
**1 onion, thinly sliced**
**50g/2oz broccoli florets**
**25g/1oz bamboo shoots**

### Sauce:

**½ tbsp light brown sugar**
**1 tbsp wine vinegar**
**125ml/4fl oz vegetable stock**
**½ tsp tomato ketchup**
**½ tbsp cornflour**

## Ingredients for 4

**350g/12oz egg noodles**
**Oil for deep fat frying**
**2 tbsp sunflower oil**
**2 cloves garlic, peeled and**
   **chopped**
**1 carrot, sliced into**
   **matchsticks**
**1 green pepper, thinly sliced**
**1 onion, thinly sliced**
**100g/4oz broccoli florets**
**50g/2oz bamboo shoots**

### Sauce:

**2 tbsp light brown sugar**
**2 tbsp wine vinegar**
**225ml/8fl oz vegetable stock**
**1 tsp tomato ketchup**
**1 tbsp cornflour**

1 Cook the noodles in boiling salted water for 2 minutes, drain and rinse under cold running water. Drain well in a colander.

2 Heat the oil in a wok or frying pan and stir-fry the garlic and vegetables for 3-4 minutes, stirring constantly.

3 Heat the oil in a deep-fat fryer to 180°C/350°F. Form the drained noodles into round nest shapes. Lower the nests into the hot oil in a basket in batches and deep-fry until crisp, turning them over once. Drain on kitchen paper.

4 Place the brown sugar, vinegar, stock and ketchup in a small pan. Blend the cornflour with 2 tablespoons of water and add to the pan. Heat gently until thickened, then pour over the vegetables and noodles.

# Special Mixed Vegetables

*Quick and Easy*

Chinese vegetable dishes are always colourful, crisp and quick to cook.

## Ingredients for 2

- 1 tbsp sunflower oil
- 1 clove garlic, peeled and chopped
- 1 small onion, sliced
- 1 green chilli, seeded and chopped
- 1 carrot, sliced into matchsticks
- 1/2 yellow pepper, seeded and sliced
- 50g/2oz sugarsnap peas
- 25g/1oz brown cap or oyster mushrooms, sliced
- 1 tsp cornflour
- 1 tbsp soy sauce
- 125ml/4fl oz vegetable stock

## Ingredients for 4

- 2 tbsp sunflower oil
- 1 clove garlic, peeled and chopped
- 1 medium onion, sliced
- 1 green chilli, seeded and chopped
- 2 carrots, sliced into matchsticks
- 1 yellow pepper, seeded and sliced
- 100g/4oz sugarsnap peas
- 50g/2oz brown cap or oyster mushrooms, sliced
- 2 tsp cornflour
- 2 tbsp soy sauce
- 225ml/8fl oz vegetable stock

1 Heat the oil in a wok or large frying pan, add the garlic, onion and chilli and stir-fry for 1 minute.

2 Add the carrot and pepper and stir-fry for 2 minutes to soften. Add the sugarsnap peas and mushrooms and cook for a further 2 minutes.

3 Mix the cornflour with the soy sauce and 1 tablespoon of water to a paste, then blend with the vegetable stock.

4 Pour the liquid over the vegetables and allow it to bubble up and thicken for a few moments. Stir well and serve immediately.

# Hot Mixed Vegetable Salad

*vegetarian*

Serve this light dish as a starter, or as a partner to grilled prawns.

## Ingredients for 2

**1/2 red pepper**
**1 stalk celery**
**1/2 cucumber**
**1 tbsp sunflower oil**
**1 clove garlic, peeled and chopped**
**1cm/1/2 inch root ginger, peeled and chopped**
**1 medium onion, peeled and thinly sliced**
**100g/4oz beansprouts**
**1/2 tsp salt**
**2 tsp rice vinegar**
**1 tbsp soy sauce**
**1 tsp sesame oil**
**A few drops of chilli sauce**

## Ingredients for 4

**1 red pepper**
**2 stalks celery**
**1 small cucumber**
**2 tbsp sunflower oil**
**2 cloves garlic, peeled and chopped**
**2.5cm/1 inch root ginger, peeled and chopped**
**1 large onion, peeled and thinly sliced**
**225g/8oz beansprouts**
**1 tsp salt**
**1 tbsp rice vinegar**
**2 tbsp soy sauce**
**2 tsp sesame oil**
**A dash of chilli sauce**

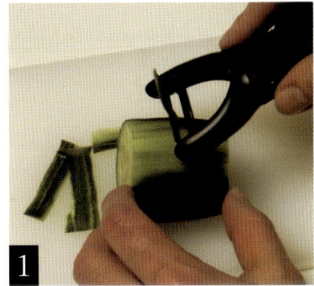

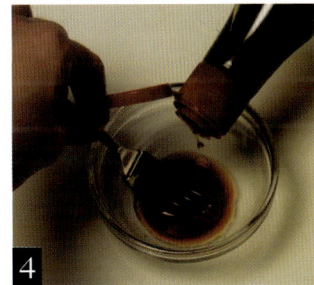

1 Remove the seeds and stalk from the pepper and cut into thin slices. Trim the celery and cut diagonally into thin strips. Peel the cucumber and cut into thin matchsticks.

2 Heat the oil in a wok or large frying pan and stir-fry the garlic, ginger and onion for 1 minute to soften.

3 Add the peppers and celery and stir-fry quickly for 30 seconds. Add the beansprouts and cucumber and stir-fry for another 30 seconds. Don't over-cook as the vegetables need to retain their crunchiness.

4 Spoon the vegetables onto a serving platter. Mix the salt, vinegar, soy sauce, sesame oil and chilli sauce together and sprinkle over the salad. Serve immediately.

# Braised Aubergines

*Hot and spicy*

Serve with flat noodles to make a perfect partner for pork dishes.

## Ingredients for 2

- 1 small aubergine
- 1 tbsp sunflower oil
- 1 clove garlic, peeled and crushed
- 2.5cm/1 inch root ginger, peeled and chopped
- 1/2 green pepper, seeded and cubed
- 1/2 red pepper, seeded and cubed
- 1 small red bird's-eye chilli, sliced
- 4 tbsp vegetable stock
- 1 tbsp yellow bean sauce
- 1/2 tsp rice vinegar
- 1/2 tsp caster sugar
- 1/2 tbsp soy sauce

## Ingredients for 4

- 1 large aubergine
- 2 tbsp sunflower oil
- 2 cloves garlic, peeled and crushed
- 2.5cm/1 inch root ginger, peeled and chopped
- 1 green pepper, seeded and cubed
- 1 red pepper, seeded and cubed
- 1 red bird's-eye chilli, sliced
- 125ml/4fl oz vegetable stock
- 2 tbsp yellow bean sauce
- 1 tsp rice vinegar
- 1 tsp caster sugar
- 1 tbsp soy sauce

1 Cut the aubergine into large cubes, sprinkle lightly with salt and leave to drain in a colander for 30 minutes. Rinse thoroughly under cold water.

2 Heat the oil in a wok or large frying pan and fry the garlic and ginger for 1 minute.

3 Add the aubergine, peppers and chilli and stir-fry for 4 minutes to brown.

4 Add the stock, yellow bean sauce, vinegar, sugar and soy sauce and stir well. Simmer over a low heat for 10 minutes until the vegetables are softened. Spoon into warmed serving bowls and garnish with coriander.

# Hot & Spicy Cucumbers

*vegetarian*

Cucumbers are never eaten raw in China and are always cooked with other, more powerful flavours.

## Ingredients for 2

- 1 medium cucumber
- 1 tsp salt
- 2 tsp sunflower oil
- 1 clove garlic, peeled and chopped
- 2 spring onions, sliced
- 1 carrot, thinly sliced
- 1 chilli, seeded and chopped
- 1 tbsp yellow bean sauce
- 3 tbsp water
- 1/2 tsp sesame oil
- 1 tbsp coriander, chopped

## Ingredients for 4

- 2 medium cucumbers
- 2 tsp salt
- 1 tbsp sunflower oil
- 2 cloves garlic, peeled and chopped
- 4 spring onions, sliced
- 2 carrots, thinly sliced
- 2 chillies, seeded and chopped
- 2 tbsp yellow bean sauce
- 6 tbsp water
- 1 tsp sesame oil
- 2 tbsp coriander, chopped

1 Peel the cucumber and cut in half lengthways. Scoop out the seeds from the centre with a teaspoon. Cut into 2.5cm/1 inch slices, sprinkle with salt and place in a colander.

2 Leave to stand for 30 minutes to drain away excess water from the cucumber. Rinse well in cold water and leave to drain.

3 Heat the oil in a wok or large frying pan and add the garlic, chilli, carrot and spring onions and stir-fry for 1 minute.

4 Add the cucumber with the yellow bean sauce and stir-fry for 30 seconds. Add the water and cook for about 4 minutes until the water evaporates. Serve sprinkled with sesame oil and chopped coriander.

# desserts

# Almond Float with Fruit

*Low Fat*

This bright dessert provides a colourful ending to any dinner party.

### Ingredients for 2
**2 tbsp powdered gelatine**
**75g/3oz caster sugar**
**300ml/¹/₂ pint milk**
**1 tsp almond essence**
**1 kiwi fruit**
**1 small mango**
**100g/4oz strawberries**

### Ingredients for 4
**4 tbsp powdered gelatine**
**175g/6oz caster sugar**
**600ml/1pt milk**
**2 tsp almond essence**
**2 kiwi fruits**
**1 mango**
**225g/8oz strawberries**

1 Blend the gelatine mixture with a small whisk.

2 Sprinkle the gelatine over 6 tablespoons of cold water in a bowl and leave to become spongy for 10 minutes. Dissolve the sugar in 175ml/6fl oz of water. Bring to the boil, then pour over the gelatine and stir until the mixture dissolves.

3 Add the milk and essence to the gelatine mixture and stir together. Pour into a 20cm/8 inch or 23cm/9 in square, shallow tin and chill in the refrigerator for 2 hours.

4 Peel the kiwi fruits and slice thinly. Cut the mango in half and remove the stone. Mark each half into cubes, push back the skin, then cut the cubes away. Remove the hulls from the strawberries and halve them or slice thinly if they are large.

5 Cut the almond jelly into 5cm/2 inch diamond shapes in the tin. Remove with a palette knife and place three diamonds on a plate with an assortment of sliced kiwis, mangoes and strawberries.

# Lychee Sorbet

No Fat

Refreshing and light, keep this sorbet in the freezer for serving after heavy or fatty dishes such as duck.

## Ingredients for 4

**450g/1lb stoned, canned lychees (drained weight)**
**150ml/¼ pint syrup from the tin**
**150ml/¼ pint water**
**50g/2oz vanilla caster sugar**
**3 drops rose water**
**4 lychees and mint sprigs to serve**

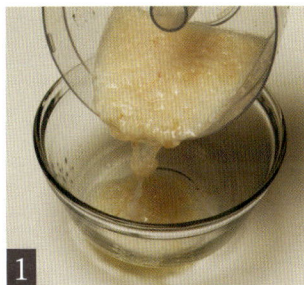

1 Put the lychees and the syrup in a food processor and blend to a smooth puree.

2 Place the water and sugar in a saucepan and heat to dissolve the sugar, then bring to the boil. Boil until a syrup forms then cool slightly.

3 Add the syrup to the puree with the rose water and stir together. Place in a freezer container and freeze for 2 hours.

4 Place the frozen pulp in the food processor and process until smooth. Re-freeze for 2-3 hours until solid. Serve in scoops in glass dishes, with mint sprigs to decorate.

# Toffee Apples

*Easy Entertaining*

The success of this dish lies in having the batter, oil and syrup all ready so that the apples can be dipped in one, then the other.

## Ingredients for 2

**2 large, firm eating apples, peeled and cored**

### Batter:
**2 tbsp plain flour**
**1/2 tbsp cornflour**
**1 egg white**
**Vegetable oil for deep-fat frying**
**100g/4oz caster sugar**
**2 tsp vegetable oil**
**1 tbsp toasted sesame seeds**

## Ingredients for 4

**4 large, firm eating apples, peeled and cored**

### Batter:
**4 tbsp plain flour**
**1 tbsp cornflour**
**2 egg whites**
**Vegetable oil for deep-fat frying**
**100g/4oz caster sugar**
**2 tsp vegetable oil**
**1 tbsp toasted sesame seeds**

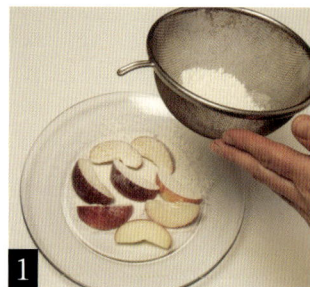

1 Cut each apple into eight slices and sprinkle each with a little of the flour. Mix the remaining flour with the cornflour and then whisk with the egg whites to make a batter.

2 Place the sugar in a heavy -based saucepan with 2 tablespoons of water and stir over a gentle heat until the sugar has completely dissolved. Add the oil, increase the heat and boil until the sugar becomes golden and caramelised. Turn off the heat.

3 Meanwhile, heat the oil in a deep-fat fryer. Coat each piece of apple in the batter and deep-fry for about 3 minutes. Remove from the oil with a slotted spoon and drain.

4 Dip the apple pieces in the caramel and serve sprinkled with toasted sesame seeds.

# Eight Treasure Rice Pudding

*Family Favourite*

This special dish is served at New Year and other celebrations in China. The eight treasures are the rice and different fruits which are supposed to keep away evil spirits.

## Ingredients for 4

175g/6oz pudding rice
25g/1oz butter
2 tbsp caster sugar
10 dried, pitted dates
50g/2oz raisins
10 glace cherries, halved
25g/1oz candied angelica, chopped

10 walnut halves
100g/4oz canned chestnut puree

### Syrup:
3 tbsp caster sugar
1 long strip of orange peel
1 tbsp cornflour

1 Butter a 900ml/1½ pint pudding basin. Put the rice in a saucepan, cover with cold water and bring to the boil. Simmer for 10-15 minutes until the water has been absorbed. Stir in the butter and sugar.

2 Coat the base and sides of the basin with a thin layer of the cooked rice. Place a circle of dates around the base of the mould. Cover this with a thin layer of rice. Continue layering the rice with the fruits, making a hollow in the centre.

3 Press the fruits into the sides of the basin so that they will show through when the pudding is turned out. Fill the centre with the chestnut puree, then finally cover with the remaining rice. Press down to flatten. Cover with foil and steam for 1 hour, then leave to stand for 10 minutes.

4 To make the syrup, dissolve the sugar in 300ml/½ pint water with the peel, then boil for 5 minutes until thick. Blend the cornflour to a paste in 2 tablespoons of water and add to the syrup. Heat until thickened. Serve the pudding cut into slices with the syrup drizzled over.

# Fruit Salad

*Quick and Easy*

This refreshing salad can be made in advance and chilled.

### Ingredients for 2

1 small orange
2 clementines
350g/12oz fresh lychees,
    peeled and stoned
½ small pineapple
3 pieces stem ginger in
    syrup
1 tbsp stem ginger syrup
    from the jar
75g/3oz physalls

### Ingredients for 4

1 large orange
4 clementines
700g/1lb 8oz fresh lychees,
    peeled and stoned
1 small pineapple
6 pieces stem ginger in
    syrup
2 tbsp stem ginger syrup
    from the jar
175g/6oz physalis

1 Squeeze the juice from the orange into a glass serving bowl and stir in the lychees.

2 Slice the pineapple. Cut away the skin and spines and remove the central core with a sharp knife. Cut into small segments and add to the bowl.

3 Peel the clementines and remove any white pith. Divide into segments and cut away any further pith and membranes. Add to the salad in the bowl.

4 Slice the ginger into thin matchsticks and add to the bowl with the syrup. Chill for 30 minutes. Peel back the papery skins from the physalis and arrange in the bowl or, alternatively, on plates with the salad.

# Mango Fool

*Quick and Easy*

Light and creamy, this simple dessert could not be quicker to make.

### Ingredients for 2

**225g/8oz ripe mangoes**
**1 tbsp fresh orange juice**
**1 tbsp vanilla caster sugar**
**150ml/¼ pint whipping**
   **cream**
**Orange twists to decorate**

### Ingredients for 4

**450g/1lb ripe mangoes**
**1 tbsp fresh orange juice**
**2 tbsp vanilla caster sugar**
**300ml/½ pint whipping**
   **cream**
**Orange twists to decorate**

1 Cut a large slice from one side of the mango, near to the stone, then repeat on the other side. Cut the flesh in the slices lengthways then crossways, leaving it on the skin. Push the skin inside out to expose the cubes of fruit. Cut the cubes away from the skin. Cut any remaining flesh away from the stone.

2 Place the fruit in a food processor with the orange juice and blend to a puree. Place in a bowl and stir in the sugar.

3 Whip the cream until it forms soft peaks, then fold in the mango puree.

4 Spoon into glass dishes and chill for 30 minutes before serving.

# Almond Cookies

*Easy Entertaining*

The Chinese do not make many cakes, but these little snacks are a popular choice for serving with tea or desserts.

## Makes 24

**100g/4oz unsalted butter**
**100g/4oz caster sugar**
**1 egg, beaten**
**A few drops of almond essence**
**150g/5oz self-raising flour**
**25g/1oz ground almonds**
**Blanched almonds**

1 Preheat the oven to 180°C/350°F/Gas 4. Line two baking sheets with non-stick baking paper. Beat the butter and sugar together until light and fluffy.

2 Beat in half the egg with the almond essence. Add the flour and almonds and work by hand into a soft dough. Shape the mixture into 24 small pieces.

3 Roll each piece into a ball and place on the baking sheets spaced well apart. Flatten each slightly, then press an almond on top of each one.

4 Beat the reserved egg with 2 tablespoons of cold water and brush over each cookie. Bake for 12-15 minutes until pale golden and crisp.

# Kumquat & Orange Salad

No Fat

Oranges hold a special place in China and are a sign of prosperity and good luck. They are always eaten at Chinese New Year.

## Ingredients for 2
**225g/8oz kumquats**
**50g/2oz granulated sugar**
**150ml/¹/₄ pint water**
**50g/2oz preserved ginger in
    syrup**
**2 large oranges**

## Ingredients for 4
**450g/1lb kumquats**
**100g/4oz granulated sugar**
**300ml/¹/₂ pint water**
**100g/4oz preserved ginger in
    syrup**
**4 large oranges**

1 Wash the kumquats and remove the stalks. Place the sugar and water in a saucepan and heat gently to dissolve the sugar. Bring to the boil and simmer for a few minutes to make a clear syrup.

2 Add the kumquats and poach them in the syrup for 15 minutes until tender. Leave to cool in the syrup.

3 Cut the kumquats in half and chop the ginger into small pieces. Place both in a bowl with the syrup and chill for 2-4 hours.

4 Peel the oranges and remove any white pith and seeds. Divide into segments or slice the oranges thinly. Arrange on a plate with the kumquats and syrup.

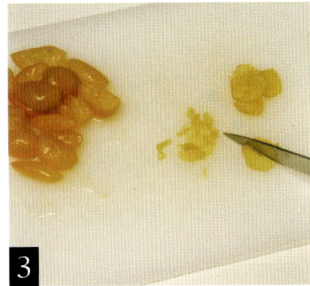

# Poached Spicy Pears

*No Fat*

Chinese cuisine does not include many desserts, but fresh fruit dishes are always popular.

### Ingredients for 2
2 large dessert pears
15ml/$^1/_4$ pint orange juice
1 tbsp caster sugar
1 cinnamon stick

### Ingredients for 4
4 large dessert pears
300ml/$^1/_2$ pint orange juice
2 tbsp caster sugar
2 cinnamon sticks

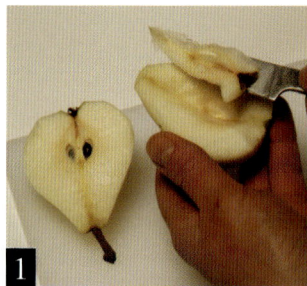

1 Peel the pears and cut in half. Scoop out the cores with a sharp knife.

2 Place the orange juice and sugar in a heavy-based pan and heat gently to dissolve the sugar.

3 Add the cinnamon sticks and the pears and simmer for 10 minutes or until the pears are tender.

4 Allow two pear halves per person with the syrup drizzled over. Serve hot or chill for 1 hour and serve cold.

# Stuffed Ginger Lychees

## Easy Entertaining

This dessert looks sophisticated, but is really very easy to make.

### Ingredients for 2

225g/8oz fresh lychees or
   200g/7oz can lychees,
   drained
25g/1oz preserved ginger
   in syrup
2 tbsp syrup from the jar
1 large orange
225g/8oz ripe papaya

### Ingredients for 4

450g/1lb fresh lychees or
   400g/14oz can lychees,
   drained
50g/2oz preserved ginger
   in syrup
4 tbsp syrup from the jar
1 large orange
450g/1lb ripe papaya

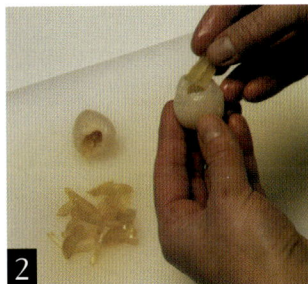

1 Peel and remove the stones from the lychees, if using fresh fruit.

2 Cut the ginger into matchsticks and press into the central cavity of each lychee. Divide the fruits between the serving plates.

3 Peel the zest from the orange and cut into thin matchsticks with a sharp knife. Sprinkle the strips over the lychees. Squeeze out the juice and mix with the syrup from the jar of ginger.

4 Slice the papaya in half and scoop out the seeds. Peel away the skin and place the flesh in a food processor with the orange juice and ginger. Process to a puree and divide the coulis between the serving plates. Chill for 30 minutes before serving.

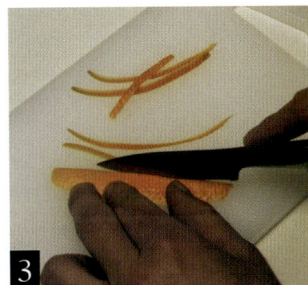

# index

# credits & acknowledgements

I would like to thank Oxo for supplying their Real Stock for photography (www.realstockbyoxo.co.uk) and to Harrison Fisher and Co (www.premiercutlery.co.uk) for supplying the knives and some of the small kitchen utensils used in the step-by-step pictures.

Thanks to Mandy Phipps for her creative food styling, and to photographers Colin Bowling and Paul Forrester at Britannia Studios.